For
GOOD
Or
BAD

People of the Cimarron Country

For
GOOD
Or
BAD

People of the Cimarron Country

Compiled and Edited
by
Stephen Zimmer

A Philmont Scout Ranch Book
from

SUNSTONE
PRESS

For two riders of the Cimarron Country
Les Davis and Jiggs Porter

All photographs, unless indicated,
courtesy of Philmont Museum.

Sunstone books may be purchased for educational, business, or sales promotional use.
For information please write: Special Markets Department, Sunstone Press, P.O. Box
2321, Santa Fe, New Mexico 87504-2321.

10 9 8 7 6 5 4 3 2

Library of Congress Cataloging in Publication Data:
    For good or bad: people of the Cimarron country / compiled and edited by Stephen
Zimmer.
        p. cm.
    Includes bibliographical references and index.
    ISBN: 0-86534-292-X
    1. Pioneers—New Mexico—Colfax County Biography. 2. Colfax County (N.M.) Bi-
ography. 3. Frontier and pioneer life—New Mexico—Colfax County. I. Zimmer, Stephen,
1951–.
    F802 . C7F67 1999
    978 . 9'22—dc   99-23075
                                                      CIP

Published by   SUNSTONE PRESS
                    Post Office Box 2321
                    Santa Fe, NM 87504-2321 / USA
                    (505) 988-4418 / *orders only* (800) 243-5644
                    FAX (505) 988-1025

INTRODUCTION

Cimarron lies nestled on the east side of the Cimarron Range of the Sangre de Cristo Mountains in northeastern New Mexico. In the 1870s Cimarron earned a bad reputation as a wild and woolly frontier town. The reputation resulted primarily from an unfortunate land grant war by which the little settlement justifiably earned its name—Cimarron—meaning wild, untamed, or unbroken.

Cimarron in the 1870s.

The town got its start when frontiersman Lucien Maxwell moved his ranch from the Santa Fe Trail settlement of Rayado north to the Cimarron River in 1857. A year later, the former mountain man purchased half of the Mexican land grant of which the ranch was a part from Guadalupe Miranda. Miranda had originally acquired the land in partnership with Maxwell's father-in-law, Carlos Beaubien, in 1841. Because of ambiguities in Mexican law, Maxwell was unclear as to the exact boundaries of the grant. The resulting dispute was the cause of many troubles for subsequent owners.

Maxwell's ranch slowly became populated by herders and farmers who took care of his stock and cultivated his fields. Because it was the only settlement in the northeastern part of New Mexico Territory, the ranch became a frequent stopover for traders traveling the mountain branch of the Santa Fe Trail. Wagons filled with goods were unloaded almost daily and Maxwell's store became the commercial center of the region.

In the early 1860s Maxwell built a stone grist mill to grind the harvest from his fields. Aside from processing flour for his employees, the mill provided rations for Jicarilla Apache and Ute Indians.

Jicarilla Apaches receiving rations from Lucien Maxwell's grist mill in the late 1860s.

Maxwell entertained many visitors at the ranch nestled on the eastern edge of the Sangre de Cristo Mountains. Many were former trapping and trading associates. Foremost among them was Kit Carson. With Carson, Maxwell had been a member of two of John C. Fremont's 1840s exploring expeditions into the Far West. Maxwell and Carson had also been partners on the Rayado Ranch. Other visitors, such as Dick Wootton, William Bent, Tom Boggs, Ceran St. Vrain and Col. Henry Inman, also spent the night reliving old glories at Maxwell's adobe home on the Cimarron.

Activity escalated at Maxwell's ranch when gold was discovered near Baldy Mountain in 1867. Thereafter, prospectors frequented the ranch as they outfitted at Maxwell's store before heading for the gold fields. Maxwell also invested in mining and although he was well rewarded for the effort, he was unable to control the many miners who prospected on the grant. Having acquired Beaubien's share of the grant in 1864, Maxwell reluctantly decided to sell his frontier empire in 1870.

Miners working the Black Horse Mine in the Baldy country.

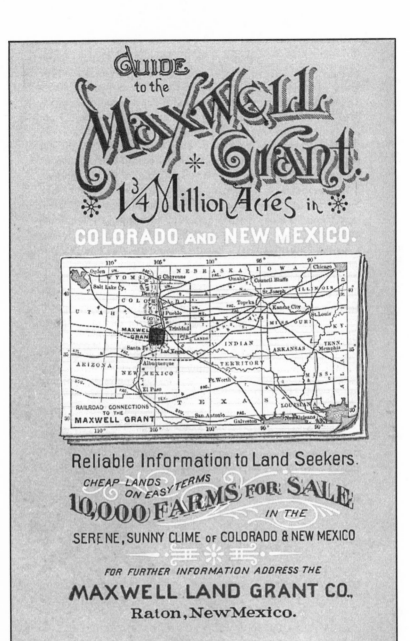

Maxwell Land Grant Company promotional brochure.

The grant was eventually purchased by a Dutch holding company organized as the Maxwell Land Grant Company. Their object was to sell grazing and farm land, mine gold and run cattle. The company immediately encountered resistance from miners and others who had previously settled on Maxwell's ranch but who did not hold title to their claims. Where Maxwell had allowed many to live and work on the grant, the Land Grant Company considered most residents squatters and insisted that they purchase title or vacate their homes. On their side, the miners and settlers believed that they resided on public domain outside the Maxwell Grant which they believed to include no more than one hundred thousand acres.

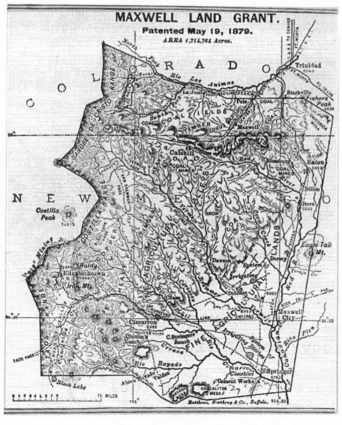

The Beaubien and Miranda or Maxwell Land Grant.

The dispute escalated into a violent conflict that became known as the Colfax County War. Grant officials attempted to force the supposed squatters to settle up their claims or move. The settlers were led by a campaigning Methodist minister, Reverend F.J. Tolby, who relentlessly championed their cause. However, when the devoted parson was mysteriously murdered in Cimarron Canyon in September of 1875, his death touched off violence that pervaded the region for the next fifteen years.

In part because of Tolby's death, another minister, Reverend Oscar P. McMains, took up the crusade to fight the grant company. Despite his efforts, the United States Supreme Court confirmed the right of the company to nearly two million acres of land in a decision rendered on April 18, 1887. Peace gradually came as the dissenting ranchers, farmers and miners either bought their land or sold the improvements and left.

Maxwell Cattle Company roundup in the 1880s.

Thereafter, the area around Cimarron became primarily a stock raising country. Foremost among the ranchers were Frank and Charles Springer who started the CS Ranch in 1873. Frank Springer had gained public attention by successfully arguing the land grant company's case before the Supreme Court.

After the turn of the century, residents of the Cimarron country benefited from the arrival of railroads that allowed them to transport cattle, gold ore, coal and mine timbers. The sleepy town prospered.

St. Louis, Rocky Mountain, & Pacific train at the depot in Cimarron.

However, it did not outlive its reputation. For better or worse, writers began recounting the events of Cimarron's turbulent years almost before the last gun shots were fired. Some embellished the truth both in book and periodical form in an attempt to make a good story even better.

Tourist brochures found in the motels and cafes of Cimarron tell of notable Western characters who graced its streets and saloons during its turbulent days. If these leaflets are to be believed, these personalities comprise a veritable Who's Who of desperados, lawmen and other figures of Western legend. According to these materials, Wyatt Earp, Billy the Kid, Butch Cassidy, Jesse James and his killer, Bob Ford, all took drinks in the St. James Hotel and shot up the town during their visits.

Historians, however, have found little verification that these men made stops in Cimarron. More likely, the town's publicists have simply taken license in an effort to lure visitors into stopping overnight.

Setting aside the exaggeration of historical events, it is nonetheless clear that Cimarron has endured enough civil disturbance to warrant "shoot-'em-up" status by the best of Hollywood standards. The individuals involved may not have enjoyed the notoriety of better known desperados but their exploits were sufficiently nefarious nonetheless.

Despite the gun slinging, card playing and whiskey drinking elements that have drawn so much attention, Cimarron boasted innumerable citizens who helped make it an agreeable place to raise children, go to church, conduct business and raise cows and horses.

Many of the good and the bad who have passed through Cimarron have been written about in popular and scholarly works. The compilation that follows represents a cross-section of writings about individuals who, for good or bad, played some part in the historical or legendary tradition of Cimarron. Others, like Frank and Charles Springer, Jesus Abreu, Brownlow Wilson, William French and countless cowboys, farmers, miners, lumbermen and merchants could have been included. Their stories simply have not been written.

Most of the people whose stories are included herein are not well known beyond the boundaries of present-day Colfax County, New Mexico. Together, however, they provide an overview of a diverse, industrious group of people, with a few hardcases thrown in, who were not unlike inhabitants of countless other Western frontier towns. Although some of the entries are better documented historically than others, all are good stories and equally important to Cimarron's tradition.

Street scene in Cimarron at the turn of the century.

The main purpose of this compilation is to present, in one volume, representative portrayals of famous, infamous and not-so-well known Cimarron personalities. Most are from out-of-print books or hard-to-find periodicals.

—Stephen Zimmer
Cimarron, New Mexico

LUCIEN MAXWELL (1818-1875)

Larry Murphy worked on the Philmont Scout Ranch staff for ten years during the 1960s. Like many who have spent summers at Philmont, Murphy developed a great interest in the history of the Cimarron country, a curiosity that led him to pursue an academic career in history. After completing a doctorate at Texas Christian University, he taught western history at several universities.

Murphy was a thorough researcher and a prolific writer who wrote in a highly readable style. His first book, *Philmont, A History of New Mexico's Cimarron Country* (1972), was an admirable effort at separating fact from local lore. Although Murphy later described his work as an exercise in popular history, the book deals more with economic development and settlement than with the sensational murders and intrigue that dominate so many accounts of the region. It was well received and remains the primary source for the history of the Cimarron country.

In 1983, Murphy wrote a biography of Lucien Maxwell that he titled *Lucien Bonaparte Maxwell, Napoleon of the Southwest*. It is more scholarly in approach and effectively documents the facts of Maxwell's life and juxtaposes them against the legendary portrayals left by other writers. A more recent biography, *Lucien Maxwell: Villain or Visionary* by Harriet Freiberger (1999) gives new insights into this controversial figure.

Apart from these biographies, readers may wish to peruse novelist Harvey Fergusson's fictional treatment of the frontiersman's life, *Grant of Kingdom* (1950).

Lucien Maxwell, Master of the Cimarron.

Master of the Cimarron: Lucien B. Maxwell

by Lawrence R. Murphy *New Mexico Historical Review,*
Vol. 55, No.1, January, 1980, pp. 5–23

Few nineteenth century New Mexicans achieved the lasting renown of Cimarron rancher Lucien B. Maxwell. As owner of one of the largest and most hotly disputed Mexican land grants in the Southwest, he controlled vast properties in the northeastern section of the territory and southern Colorado. The location of an Indian agency at his ranch provided him with an assured market for agricultural produce, increased his wealth, and gave him considerable influence in Indian policy decisions. With the discovery of gold on the slopes of nearby Baldy Mountain, Maxwell's ranch became the center of a short-lasted rush of prospectors into the Sangre de Cristos, and Maxwell himself controlled mines which made him extremely rich. Most of all, however, what made Maxwell famous were his extensive Cimarron mansion, his renowned hospitality to visitors, and his colorful personality. It is these aspects of his varied career upon which this article focuses.

Nearly twenty years of frontier experience preceded Maxwell's arrival on the Cimarron. Born in Kaskaskia, Illinois, September 14, 1818, he was the son of an Irish-born storekeeper; his mother was the daughter of Pierre Menard, a highly successful trader and first Lieutenant Governor of Illinois. Lucien probably headed west soon after the death of his father in an 1833 cholera epidemic, and by the mid-1830s was working for Bent, St. Vrain, and Company in their trading posts along the South Platte and the Arkansas. In the years that followed, he became close friends with Kit Carson, accompanied John C. Fremont on two of his western expeditions, and, most important, married Luz Beaubien, whose Canadian-born father, Charles, had become one of the leading merchants in Taos and co-owner of a Mexican land grant on the eastern side of the Sangre de Cristo mountains. Following the death of Beaubien's son in the Taos revolt, Maxwell moved to the banks of the Rayado, where he established on behalf of his father-in-law the first permanent settlement in that part of New Mexico.

By the mid-1850s Maxwell was ready to move. For close to two decades he had served apprenticeship on the frontier, learning important skills from the likes of Fremont, Carson, and Beaubien. He had come west as a poor teenager and adroitly accumulated the profits of several successful business ventures. Rayado, he recognized, was no place to build his empire. The settlement had been founded under Beaubien's auspices, and whoever lived there would inevitably fall under his shadow. Moreover, once the danger of Indian attack subsided, wagon trains often cut directly across the plains, east of what became known as Kit Carson Mesa, missing Rayado entirely. An old trail across the mountains to Taos fell into disuse as other more direct routes developed. And perhaps then as is occasionally still the case, a drought revealed how fickle a stream the Rayado could be; without water, crops died, and livestock had to be sold.

The banks of the Cimarron River, ten miles to the north of Rayado, offered much better possibilities. It was a larger and stronger stream, better fed and more reliable. The Cimarron poured out of the mountains through a narrow, picturesque canyon onto a broad, fertile plain, protected from winter storms by the surrounding low hills. Here was ample room for thousands of sheep and cattle to graze and for vast fields of corn, wheat, and hay to grow. The Jicarilla Apache, who had once camped along its banks, were largely gone, and, as Surveyor John G. Parke had noted, the area had many strategic advantages in case of attack by the Plains Indians. Stages running between the eastern settlements and New Mexico often stopped here for the night, and the Cimarron River had cut a fairly direct—although as yet largely undeveloped—route toward Taos. With sufficient energy and capital, the area could be developed into an important crossroads in northern New Mexico.

Exactly when Maxwell moved his headquarters to the Cimarron is uncertain. Farmers had lived there at least seasonally since the mid-1840s, and at first the Cimarron must have been one of several locations where herders watched Maxwell's herds of cattle and sheep. Probably by the mid-1850s, some of the Mexican-Americans who had farmed at Rayado moved there and began building a substantial residence and other buildings for Maxwell. According to family tradition, Lucien talked about his plans for the Cimarron place during an 1858 visit to Kaskaskia. One of his objectives in making the long trip home may well have been to purchase furniture and other goods for the new house, and probably by 1857 or 1858, he had established himself and his family at what became known as "Maxwell's Ranche."

The house which Lucien built on the Cimarron quickly became one of the best-known landmarks in northern New Mexico. One visitor characterized it as a "palace when compared to the prevailing style of architecture in that country." "Palacial for that region," observed another, while a third termed it "exceedingly comfortable." In many ways the general design of the house was reminiscent of styles prevalent at Kaskaskia when Lucien was growing up there and in particular of his grandfather Menard's spacious residence overlooking the Mississippi. "It was built like a French villa," recalled British traveler William A. Bell, "with an open court inside and a verandah, running the whole length of the building, covered by a projecting roof." There were dormered windows on the second floor, and massive brick chimneys rising above a peaked roof. Like nearly all houses in New Mexico, the edifice was built of sun-dried adobe bricks, although Lucien had white-washed the structure to give it the "appearance of a modern brick building." "It was large and roomy," recalled Colonel Henry J. Inman, a frequent visitor, "purely American in its construction."

Ruins of Maxwell's home in Cimarron.

The inside of the house, too, impressed visitors. "The rooms were large," remembered Irving Howbert, "having high ceilings finished with moulding." The main dining room, where Maxwell entertained his male visitors, was "an extended rectangular affair," which in Inman's opinion "might properly have been termed the Baronial Hall. . . . There," he reported, "Maxwell received his friends, transacted business with his vassals, and held high carnival at times." A separate dining room and parlor were provided for the women, in accordance with accepted New Mexico custom, and there were numerous sleeping rooms upstairs and down for family members, guests, and servants.

At first, perhaps before he had an opportunity to make buying trips east or to accumulate enough money to pay for expensive furnishings, many of the rooms were empty of furniture. The room Irving Howbert slept in "was carpeted but had not even a chair." In one corner stood a pile of wool mattresses and bedding which servants made into a bed at night. "So far as we saw," he went on, "there was only one room in the house that had a bedstead, and that was the one occupied by Maxwell and his wife." "I have slept on its hardwood floor," Henry Inman reminisced with the pride of one who had partaken in history, "rolled up in my blanket."

> I have sat there in the long winter evenings, when the great room was lighted only by the cheerful blaze of the crackling logs roaring up the huge throats of its two fireplaces built diagonally across opposite corners, watching Maxwell, Kit Carson, and half a dozen chiefs . . . until the glimmer of Aurora announced the advent of another day.

Later, as Lucien's wealth and his affection for the comforts of life grew, many of the rooms were elaborately decorated with "deep-piled carpets, heavy velvet draperies, gold-framed paintings." The furniture, much of which had to have been hauled across the Santa Fe trail by wagon, was "of the most massive Victorian sort." Even to the present day, no antique is more prized by the old families of northeastern New Mexico than a piece reputed to have come from the Maxwell mansion. Reportedly Lucien brought from the states four pianos, two for the first floor of the house and two more for the second. "It still seems to me," a writer who had visited the house as a child recalled after many years, "a little overdone, even now!"

The house was only one of several structures Maxwell had built on the south bank of the Cimarron. There was a large wooden barn which reminded one visitor of many he had observed in Pennsylvania. The structure may not have been entirely suited to New Mexico, for one of the Indian agents assigned to Cimarron complained of having to store his annuity goods there, mixed up with Lucien's "produce and dye stuffs," because they were subject to the destructive powers of "hundreds of industrious mice." In another smaller building two Navajo women spent their days weaving rugs on Indian style looms. Nearby was a general store, "well filled with everything necessary for a frontier man's life," supplying goods to local residents and serving as a wholesaler to a number of smaller stores in the region. The business must have been one of Lucien's more profitable activities, for, as William Hoehne, who did business there for many years, reported, a three to five hundred percent markup on merchandise was common. Later Lucien acquired a second store in Taos, purchased from a Jewish merchant named Soloman Beuthner, and run by Henry Stillman; he purchased a third store in Elizabethtown from Santa Fe businessman V.S. Shelby.

Maxwell's most ambitious building project was a massive stone mill for grinding corn and wheat into flour. Alone among his major buildings, it has survived well over a hundred years and serves today as a museum dedicated to preserving historic relics of the area. To supervise its erection, Maxwell had already hired by 1860 a Boston-born engineer, B.M. Blackmore, millwright Emory Williams, a New Yorker, and a Vermont-born mason, James Truax. The work must have gone slowly, for in mid-summer 1864, the Santa Fe *New Mexican* reported that Maxwell, whom the editor described as "one of our most prominent and successful stockmen," was building "a grist mill capable of turning out three hundred barrels of flour per day." The editor added that he welcomed "all such enterprises as indications of the onward progress of our territory." Two years later, a visitor found the "lately finished" mill to be "well and complete (sic) constructed and the machinery perfect." The excellence of the flour which he saw attested to the general success of the undertaking.

The mill, too, turned a handsome profit for Maxwell. In addition to supplying food for the Indian agency which was located at the ranch after 1861, Maxwell found ready markets for corn meal and wheat flour among the growing towns of New Mexico and Colorado and sold substantial quantities to the military headquarters at Fort Union. During the Civil War, when New Mexico was cut off for many months from trade to the south, there was a greater demand for grain, wheat, and oats than could be supplied, and prices were correspondingly inflated. As a result, as John D. Lee reported, once the mill was complete, it kept grinding "most all the time" just to keep up with the increasing demand. The mill also played an important role in the personal life of Maxwell, for it was there where his eldest daughter Virginia secretly married Indian agent A.S.B. Keyes, and enraged her disapproving father.

Besides Maxwell and his family, a substantial community grew up along the Cimarron. Except for Jesus Abreu and a man named Valdez who lived on the Rayado, all residents, recalled Albert W. Archibald, were "in some manner the tenants of Maxwell." Many resided in the Maxwell mansion itself. Rancher A.J. Calhoun recalled that whenever he was working for Lucien or during frequent visits he "lived in the house as one of the family." William R. Walker characterized the Maxwell residence as "the resort of old-timers," recalling that people came there from far and near—army officers, retired mountain men, and aging pioneers. Most area residents came originally from Rayado: Calvin Jones, who had known Maxwell since the 1840s, reported that when Lucien left the Rayado, he took "the whole outfit with him." Others came from Mora, Taos, or other towns in the region. The majority were Mexican-Americans, Sandovals and Vigils, Montoyas, Garcias, and Lobatos,—the ancestors of families whose names still fill the telephone books and adorn the rural mail boxes of northeastern New Mexico.

Irving Howbert wrote that when he visited Maxwell's "a considerable part" of the land in the area was being worked by "tenants or peons belonging to Maxwell" and estimated their total number at a thousand. John D. Lee recalled that when he first went to the Cimarron in the mid-1860s, men working under Maxwell were cultivating land along the Cimarron from the mouth of the Cimarron Canyon to the river's intersection with the Ponil, seven or eight miles, and along the Ponil from the mouth of its canyon to the Cimarron, another five or six miles. Henry Inman guessed the number of farmers at five hundred, adding that even though many were peons whose perpetual indebtedness prevented them from leaving with impunity, Maxwell was "not a harsh governor, and his people really loved him, as he was ever their friend and advisor." Benjamin H. Eaton, who later became Governor of the State of Colorado, no doubt exaggerated in describing himself as "one of Maxwell's peons," but he and many others—Anglos as well as Mexican-Americans—who began farming on Maxwell's land later became well-known and successful farmers, businessmen, or professionals.

At the bottom of the social ladder was a class of Indian slaves, nearly always women and children. During the 1850s and 1860s, Mexican-American soldiers were frequently encouraged to go to war with the Navajo Indians with promises that they could retain as personal slaves or booty any Indian captives they acquired. Maxwell, like many New Mexicans of the time, purchased Indians, who were forced to carry out the most burdensome and disagreeable tasks with no hope of freedom. In Lucien's house, for example, the government census taker found in 1850 and again a decade later, and still in 1870, Indian servants, children aged seven or nine or thirteen, whose birthplace could be given with no more certainty than "Navajo Indian country." Many took the Maxwell name, and one, Deluvina Maxwell, became famous as a friend of bandit Billy the Kid.

The importance of the Maxwell ranch received official recognition in 1861 when the United States government established a post office at what was now to be known as Cimarron. The first postmaster, not surprisingly, was Lucien Maxwell. That same year Maxwell's became a stop on the newly-established Missouri Stage Company line connecting Kansas City with Santa Fe, and in 1868 the opening of a telegraph office at Lucien's connected Cimarron directly with the East.

The empire which Lucien Maxwell established during the 1850s and 1860s was based primarily on agriculture. "The sources of his wealth," concluded Colonel Inman, "were his cattle, sheep, and the products of his area of cultivated acres—barley, oats, and corn principally. . . ." In 1864 the Santa Fe *New Mexican* reported that the grain raised at Lucien's ranch was "immense in quantity" and that Maxwell owned hundreds of cattle, mostly cows, "of improved breeds from the states." Even earlier Lucien had shown Albert W. Archibald a thoroughbred bull which he had imported at a cost of between $1,500 and $2,000. By 1866 Lucien had become interested in sheep raising. One visitor was impressed that he had bought a Spanish Merino from Vermont for the princely sum of $2,000. That might seem expensive, the writer explained, "but he is more than worth it to a man who has between twenty-five and thirty-thousand head in his flocks." Maxwell's introduction of high quality sheep, William A. Bell concluded, had "conferred a great benefit on the country." Maxwell's horses, his dogs, even his chickens, were reportedly "of the same style — the best that can be had."

As his wealth increased, Maxwell became increasingly interested in fine race horses. Irving Howbert, during his 1865 visit to the ranch, found "many fine blooded horses, several of which were noted race animals." Near the house Lucien built a race track where people from all over New Mexico witnessed matches. Another frequent visitor, Colonel Inman, reported that Lucien's "stud" included "some of the fleetest animals in the Territory," adding that "had he lived in England, he might have ruled the turf." In May of 1865 Maxwell's interest in racing led him to employ Squire T. Hart to take charge of the horses. For the next six years Hart ran Maxwell's horses against some of the best in the southwest. "He run (sic) a race every week or two," Hart recalled in his old age, "and sometimes every day." Upcoming races were frequently announced in the Pueblo, Colorado, and Santa Fe papers, often with predictions that high stakes would be bet on the outcomes.

As the Cimarron ranch became better established, visitors commonly stopped there for the night on their way between the states and Santa Fe. Some were unable to proceed because of high water, severe storms, or the fall of darkness; others deliberately took advantage of an opportunity to meet and spend an evening with a man whose fame was rapidly spreading. "A man is always welcome to Maxwell," reported one visitor, while another noted that Lucien was "one of the kindest, most generous and charitable men that lives." One of Lucien's granddaughters, Adelina Welborn, recalled years later how much Maxwell enjoyed having guests and how the housekeepers knew to keep the massive dining room table set for "dozens of people at each meal."

"Seldom," she went on, "was there a vacant place." William Walker recalled having seen as many as fifty people sitting down to a meal at Maxwell's. There were so many guests to feed that Maxwell had a beef killed every day or two and ten or twelve sheep daily.

Even unexpected visitors were treated well. William Walker recalled that once he was conducting business at Fort Union when the doctor asked him to take some medicine to Maxwell. "I got to his house about 10 o'clock at night," Walker recalled years later. Maxwell was still up, and the two men went to the barn, put up the horses, and returned to the house. Even though it was late at night, Lucien called an Indian woman to prepare supper, and after eating, the two retired to Lucien's room where they talked until midnight.

On at least one occasion, however, Maxwell's hospitality failed to live up to its usual standard. It was near midnight when the coach carrying the first Sisters of Charity to come to New Mexico arrived at Cimarron. "The people were all asleep," recalled Sister Mallon, and there were "Indians lying about." The male passengers and the driver quickly disappeared, but the nuns, not knowing whether the Indians were "savage or civilized," spent the night huddled together in the coach. The next morning, when "the people found we were there," she continued, "they invited us in to breakfast which invitation was gladly accepted." "Mrs. Maxwell treated us very kindly." The breakfast included hot green chili, the first time the sisters had encountered this New Mexico specialty. "Each one kept quiet about the hot dish until all got well burned." Then, Sister Mallon confessed with embarrassment years later, came the exclamations, "Oh, I am burning up."

There was never a charge for eating or sleeping at Maxwell's. Frequently, jockey Squire Hart recalled, when a man would ask Maxwell for his bill after an overnight stay, Lucien would reply with "What in hell have I sold to you?" "Why I have stayed all night with you, sir," came the reply. "Why I don't keep hotel," rebutted Maxwell, ending the conversation. According to another widely repeated tale, one morning after he had enjoyed food and lodging from Lucien, a well-to-do easterner approached his host to ask how much he owed. This time Maxwell, angered at the suggestion that he would take money for his hospitality, retorted that the charge would be twenty dollars. The astonished man had no choice but to pay and handed over a crisp federal greenback. With all the arrogance he could muster, Maxwell rolled up the bill, lit it at the fireplace, and used it to light his cigar.

Such displays led many of Maxwell's visitors to assess his character and demeanor. "Maxwell is a well-built man, with a fine face," reported one observer, "in which one sees the determination and self-reliance which had made him what he is, one of the most prominent men in New Mexico." A writer in the *New Mexican* added that he was "one of the most marked men, in the qualities of his character, to be found in any territory." "Nothing," he continued, "about him is narrow or diminutive. He is beloved and esteemed by his neighbors and dependents. He is a man of no personal parade. He is severely plain and unostentatious (sic)." His character was such that he would "face a regiment of tortures sooner than indulge for a moment the consciousness of mean action." "Such is Lucien B. Maxwell—he is an eminent illustration of what great energy and integrity can accomplish in this land."

William R. Walker, a soldier at Fort Union during the 1860s and a frequent visitor to Maxwell's, estimated that Lucien's influence extended "all over New Mexico, more or less, at least 100 miles around him." "What was it," a questioner probed, "that enabled him to wield such power and influence?" "His generosity, hospitality, and disposition to do what was right by everybody and to treat everybody right, and his known bravery and manly way of dealing with everybody," Walker continued, won him "respect and confidence." But there was more: Maxwell's "firmness of will." "Where his mind was set on accomplishing an object," Walker continued, "there was nothing to prevent him from attempting to carry it out regardless of danger or cost or anything that stood in his way." "People looked up to Maxwell as a kind of prince because he owned his grant property," reported another observer, adding that he was the kind of man who would have been a leader "if he had not had an acre of land." "They generally sought his advice."

Other stories recounted Lucien's generosity. Maurice LeDuc, an aging fur trapper, was living at the Cimarron in 1866 or 1867 when he became ill. Hopeful that the waters at Las Vegas Hot Springs could cure him, he helped himself to one of Maxwell's strongest burros, packed his few possessions aboard, and without asking permission or saying a word to Maxwell headed south to Las Vegas where he found a room and began daily visits to the springs. One day he heard that Lucien was staying at one of the town's hotels. According to the report of the man with whom LeDuc was staying, he "buckled on an old single-barrelled pistol that he had, put a knife in his belt and went over to the hotel." Coming up to Maxwell from the back, his right hand crossed to his pistol, he "struck an attitude, and shouted 'Hulloa, Maxwell.'" Lucien turned, recognized LeDuc, and laughed. "Maybe you think I stole your burro," said Maurice, adding that Maxwell was welcome to take the animal back. "You keep the burro, Maurice, he's yours," came the response; "I'll give him to you, and if there's anything else you want, just let me know." Anytime he got tired of Las Vegas, Maxwell encouraged LeDuc to come back to his house to stay. "Just make yourself at home, and stay there as long as you want to."

Such generosity reflected only one side of Maxwell's personality, however, for, probably unrevealed to most of those who knew him only on the basis of brief and infrequent visits to the Cimarron mansion, Lucien could also be brutal. Inman recorded a revealing story about Maxwell's handling of money. It seems that despite the fact that he often kept large accumulations of gold, silver, greenbacks, and government securities in his house, Maxwell refused to acquire a safe and kept all his cash in the bottom drawer of a dresser. When Inman questioned the safety of such an insecure place, Maxwell "only smiled, while a strange resolute look flashed from his dark eyes, as he said: 'God help the man who attempted to rob me and I knew him.'"

Others perceived the same determination. "He was a man

that nothing in the world would prevent him from accomplishing what he undertook to do," testified William R. Walker, "in fact no one ever dared to . . . stand in the way of anything that he started to accomplish." Squire Hart, another Maxwell confidant, reckoned that it was "not safe for a man to oppose him." "I mean," he explained, "I think he would be a dangerous man to oppose. . . ." William Hoehne, a Trinidad businessman, had heard similar reports. "His reputation was when he undertook anything he would carry it out, whether right or wrong." "I never saw the man in all my life," concluded pioneer Jacob Beard, who knew Maxwell for years, "that wielded as much influence over the community, people of all classes and kinds, ages and sexes, as he."

Moreover, Maxwell carried out such threats often enough to be taken seriously. Calvin Jones recalled that "his power was just as if he owned the whole outfit, the same as a man who owned slaves in the south before the war." To illustrate his point, Jones recalled a typical incident:

If a Mexican servant didn't suit him or did anything against his orders, he took a board or a plank or anything he could get hold of, and whipped him with it. I knew him to tie up one man, a Mexican, and shave off the side of his head close to the skin with a butcher knife, then he struck him fifteen or twenty lashes with a cowhide, and told him if he ever caught him on the place again, he would kill him. Some twelve or fifteen years (later), he came back with a bunch of stolen horses, and Maxwell did kill him.

Moreover, Maxwell saw himself as the arbiter of what he defined as justice. He once told Squire Hart that when two Mexicans sued one another, "he made both tell their stories, and then he would settle it right there, and made them stand for it." Another time two men broke into Maxwell's store and stole several hundred dollars worth of goods, together with a prized horse. A private posse sent after the bandits caught one of them trying to sell the loot near Rayado and returned him to the Cimarron. Lucien reportedly locked a forty-pound log chain around the unfortunate's neck and locked him in a cellar. Two days later, during which the man had been allowed neither food nor water, Maxwell exclaimed, "I forgot my prisoner," and called on his employees to produce the accused. Maxwell ordered him stripped naked, tied to a post, and administered twenty-five lashes with a cowhide whip. Lucien became irritated because the hide had not been laid on with sufficient vigor, and ordered that the prisoner be released and the whipper stripped and tied. "I will show you how to whip a thief," he lectured, striking the man fourteen or fifteen times until he fainted. "Now when I put you to whip a man," he admonished after the man had revived, "I want you to do it as I whipped you."

Nor did Maxwell tolerate interference from law enforcement agencies. An Indian servant who had belonged to the Bents lived at Maxwell's following the death of his master. During a visit to Taos the man "got in a row" and cut several men quite seriously. When a Taos constable appeared at Maxwell's to arrest the Indian, however, Lucien refused to turn him over, allegedly shooting his pistol "off in the man's face and around his head." He "punched him around with it," an observer reported, "and told him to go back and tell the justice to come after him himself, and not to send a constable, as no man could take a man out of his possession."

Explaining Maxwell's seemingly enigmatic character is difficult until it is recalled that accounts praising his generosity and kindness generally came from Anglos whom Lucien was entertaining and upon whom he looked with respect, even awe, when they visited his home. He was a gracious host to them and no doubt endeavored mightily to show his generosity and kindness. On the other hand, those who suffered his tyranny were Hispanics, usually poor farmers using Maxwell's land in exchange for a share of the proceeds or peons whose indebtedness left them few options. Maxwell expected them to obey his every word, to accept his supremacy without question. "What was Mr. Maxwell's reputation among the Mexicans, generally in northern New Mexico?" an attorney asked Calvin Jones. ". . . they feared him as being a blood-thirsty, overbearing man," came the response. "Did Maxwell intimidate people?" William Hoehne was asked. "He was king of that whole country," he answered, "and had Indians and Mexicans just to do what he bid them to." Just how much influence did he exercise? "He had perfect control," recalled Daniel Taylor.

Even generosity on the part of a Mexican-American could be dangerous. On one occasion Maxwell sent a box containing seven or eight thousand dollars east on the stage. The box somehow fell off and was found by a Mexican who came to Lucien to ask if it was his. "What box?" asked Maxwell. "Containing money and checks for large amount; here it is," the man replied. Rather than show gratefulness, however, Maxwell pulled twenty-five cents from his pocket and offered it to the man. "Here; go and buy a rope and hang yourself," he reportedly told the man. "If you found a box like that you ought to know enough to keep it."

By the late 1860s, Maxwell found it increasingly difficult to maintain the level of control he desired. Beginning in 1866 thousands of gold-seekers intruded into the Cimarron region. Few were willing to take advice from Maxwell, and many openly ignored his orders either to leave the grant or sign leases. Business affairs became increasingly complex, taxing Maxwell's financial acumen and forcing him to rely on outsiders for advice and assistance. Moreover, the presence of Utes and Apaches at the Cimarron agency created continuing tension between settlers and Indians. "I am tired of this place from the Indians and the new-comers on the land," he told Maurice Brunswick, whom he offered to sell "everything I have got" for $200,000.

Brunswick showed no serious interest, but throughout 1869 Maxwell conferred with other, wealthier investors. Late in May he signed an option with Coloradans Jerome B. Chaffee, George M Chilcott, and Charles F. Holly. Early in 1870, having found potential purchasers in Britain, the trio completed the purchase and transferred their rights to what was called the Maxwell Land Grant and Railway Company. Soon Maxwell left Cimarron, moving his family and many of the Mexican-Americans and Indians who had worked for him to a new ranch at the abandoned Fort Sumner Indian reservation in southeastern New Mexico. He remained there until his death July 25, 1875.

The fifteen years during which Lucien Maxwell reigned as master of the Cimarron constitutes an important transitional phase of New Mexico territorial history. In many ways, his success epitomized the opportunities open to ambitious, hard-working, imaginative individuals on a rapidly developing frontier. Within a few years he had founded and enlarged a new town, seen thousands of acres come into agricultural production, and begun to exploit the rich natural resources of the area. But Lucien Maxwell's life also reveals a darker side of New Mexico history. The forces of institutionalized government and law enforcement not having yet established their supremacy, men like Maxwell could exercise excessive personal power. He became the law and enjoyed the opportunity to oppress those with whom he came into contact. And too often his will was exercised largely against Mexican-Americans, revealing ethnic prejudices which persisted for generations after Maxwell's death.

KIT CARSON (1809–1868)

More than fifty biographies and novels have been written about the life of Christopher "Kit" Carson. To this point, the definitive study remains Thelma Guild and Harvey Carter's *Kit Carson: A Pattern for Heroes* (1984). Numerous fictional and historical portrayals have appeared before and since.

Carson was illiterate, able only to write his name. Fortunately, he dictated certain details of his life in 1856. Those memoirs were expanded upon by Dr. DeWitt C. Peters who published the first Carson biography under the title *The Life and Adventures of Kit Carson, the Nestor of the Rocky Mountains, from Facts Narrated by Himself* (1858).

Harvey Carter annotated Carson's memoirs in *Dear Old Kit* (1968). This edition is especially useful because it provides supporting documentation to illuminate a near exact transcription of the original text.

Carson was a resident in the Cimarron country while partnered with Maxwell in the early 1850s at Rayado Ranch. He moved to Taos in early 1854 to become United States Indian Agent for the Moache Utes, although he frequently visited Maxwell on the Cimarron Ranch thereafter. What follows is an excerpt from Carter's transcription that details Carson's adventures while on the Rayado.

Kit Carson about the time he lived at Rayado.

On the Rayado

from 'Dear Old Kit': The Historical Christopher Carson,
by Harvey Lewis Carter,
Norman: University of Oklahoma Press, 1968, pp. 123–133

In April, Mr. Maxwell and I concluded to make a settlement on the Rayado. We had been leading a roving life long enough and now was the time, if ever, to make a home for ourselves and children. We were getting old and could not expect to remain any length of time able to gain a livelihood as we had been [for] such a number of years. Arrived at Rayado, commenced building and making improvements, and were in a way of becoming prosperous.

Ruins of Carson's rancho on the Rayado.

In October, the train of Mr. White was attacked by the Jicarilla Apache Indians. He was killed and his wife and child taken prisoner. A command was organized in Taos, Leroux and

Fisher as guides. When they reached Rayado, I was employed as one of the guides. We marched to where the depredation had been committed, then took their trail. I was the first man that found the camp where the murder had been committed. Found trunks that were broken open, harness cut, etc., everything destroyed that the Indians could not carry with them. We followed them some ten or twelve days. It was the most difficult trail that I ever followed. As they would leave the camps, they, in numbers from one to two, went in different directions, to meet at some appointed place. In nearly every camp we would find some of Mrs. White's clothing, which was the cause of renewed energy on our part to continue the pursuit.

We finally came in view of the Indian Camp. I was in advance, started for their camp, calling to the men to follow. The comdg. officer ordered a halt, none then would follow me. I was informed that Leroux, the principal guide, told the officer in command to halt, that the Indians wished to have a parley. The Indians, seeing that the troops did not intend to charge on them, they commenced packing up in all haste. When the halt was ordered, the comdg. officer was shot; the ball passing through his coat, gauntlets that were in his pockets, shirts, and to the skin, doing no serious damage, only making him a little sick at the stomach. The gauntlets saved his life, leaving to the service of his country one more gallant officer. As soon as he recovered from the shock given him by the ball, he ordered the men to charge, but the order was too late for the desired effect. There was only one Indian in the camp; he, swimming into the river hard by, was shot. In about 200 yards, pursuing the Indians, the body of Mrs. White was found, perfectly warm, had not been killed more than five minutes — shot through the heart with an arrow. She evidently knew that some one was coming to her rescue. She did not see us, but it was apparent that she was endeavoring to make her escape when she received the fatal shot.

I am certain that if the Indians had been charged immediately on our arrival, she would have been saved. The Indians did not know of our approach and perhaps, not paying any particular watch of her, she could [have] run towards us, the Indians fearing to pursue. She could not possibly have lived long, for the treatment she had received from the Indians was so brutal and horrible that she could possibly last but a short period. Her life, I think, should never be regretted by her friends. She is surely far more happy in heaven, with her God, than among friends of this earth.

I do not wish to be understood as attaching any blame to the officer in command or the principal guide. They acted as they thought best for the purpose of saving the life of Mrs. White. We merely differed in opinion at the time. But I have no doubt that they now can see that if my advice had been taken, the life might have been saved, for at least a short period, of the much lamented Mrs. White.

We, however, captured all their baggage and camp equipage—many running off without any of their clothing—and some animals. We pursued the Indians for about six miles on a level prairie. One Indian was killed and two or three Indians taken prisoner. I have much regretted the failure of the attempt to save the life of so greatly esteemed and respected a lady. In camp was found a book, the first of the kind I had ever seen, in which I was made a great hero, slaying Indians by the hundred, and I have often thought that as Mrs. White would read the same, and knowing that I lived near, she would pray for my appearance and that she would be saved. I did come, but had not the power to convince those that were in command over me to pursue my plan for her rescue. They would not listen to me and they failed. I will say no more regarding the matter, attach no blame to any particular person, for I presume the consciences of those that were the cause of the failure have severely punished them ere this.

We returned and arrived at Taos in November. On the return we had the severest snow storm that I ever experienced. Had one man frozen to death. We were trying to make Barclay's fort on the Mora but, on account of the wind, we could not keep to our course, but happily arrived at some timber near Las Vegas. I learned that in the same storm many of the Indians that we had been pursuing perished. After the storm we went in to Las Vegas. Captain Judd was in command of the post and from there the command marched for Taos and I proceeded to Rayado, where I remained till Spring.

During the winter there was a detachment of ten dragoons commanded by Leigh Holbrook stationed at the Rayado. Sometime during the month of March, a party of Indians came and attacked the rancho that was about two miles distant where we had our animals that were gentle kept to graze. There were two men were in charge; both were severely wounded. One, however, made his way to the Rayado and gave the report. The Dragoons, three Americans, and myself immediately saddled up and proceeded to the Rancho. It was night when we arrived. Remained until morning, then took the trail of the animals that was driven off, followed it at a gallop for 25 miles and discovered, at a distance, the Indians. During the pursuit, some of our animals gave out and were left on the trail.

We approached the Indians cautiously and, when close, charged them; killed five, the other four made their escape. We recovered the stolen animals, with the exception of four, and then returned. Two of the men with me at the time [have] since [been] killed by the same tribe of Indians; Sergt. Holbrook, a gallant and brave soldier, was killed in the battle of Ceneguilla in 1854, and William New, a brave and experienced trapper, was killed at the Rayado a few months after our pursuit of [the] Indians that had stolen the animals from the Rayado.

On the 5th May 1850, Tim Goodel and I started to Fort Laramie with forty or fifty head of mules and horses to trade with the emigrants. Arrived about the first of June, remained about a month, disposed of our animals to good advantage. Then we separated, Goodel going to California, I for home. Arrived at the Greenhorn, a tributary of the Arkansas, had with me one Mexican boy. I learned there that the Apaches were on the road which I had to travel, watching it for the purpose of murdering those that might passs. I remained about six days to recruit my animals; I could get no one to accompany me but one man, Charles Kinney, and then started.

The first night I travelled about forty miles through the mountain[s], reached the River Trinchero. Had the animals concealed in the brush, some distance from the road, and I ascended the highest cottonwood tree for the purpose of watching for the Indians. I remained in that position during the entire day. Sometimes I would fall asleep, and nearly fall, but would recover in time and continue my watch. Near evening I saw a large body of Indians about one half mile distant. They had not as yet discovered our trail. I descended the tree. We saddled up, and proceeded on our journey, keeping in the brush some distance of[f] the road till dark. Then I took the road and travelled to Red River, got there at daylight in the morning, and that evening went to Taos. Remained a few days and departed for the Rayado.

During my absence the Indians had run off every head of stock on the Rayado. Troops were stationed there at the time, but the Indians came in such force that they feared to attack them. Shortly afterwards, there was a command sent in pursuit, commanded by Major Grier. They killed some of the Indians and recovered all the stock except that which had been killed by the Indians.

I remained at Rayado till fall, nothing having transpired of any moment except my following of an American that had organized a party for the purpose of murdering, on the plains, Mr. Saml. Weatherhead and Mr. Elias Brevort, that were supposed to have a large amount of money. Fox was the name of their leader. The object of the party was discovered by Fox, when in Taos, trying to get a man to join him. He stated to him that which was to be done. He refused to go, and, when he thought Fox had gone sufficient distance not to be apprehended, he stated what Fox had informed him.

Lieut. Taylor, 1st Dragoons, was in Taos at the time [and] came to me saying that he wished Fox apprehended for debt and requested me to pursue him for that purpose. I refused. Then he stated the true cause of his wishing him apprehended, which informed that he [Fox] and a party of men were travelling in company with Weatherhead and Brevort, and that it was their intention to murder them as soon as they reached the Cimarron, then go to Texas. I immediately agreed to go, when I knew their object. Ten dragoons was given me. We marched on till one o'clock that night. Met Capt. Ewell in command of recruits enroute for New Mexico. Stated to him the object of [my] journey. He then joined me with twenty-five men.

Came to the camp of Mr. Weatherhead and Brevort, entered it cautiously, arrested Fox, remained there that night. Capt. Ewell then took charge of Fox and returned to his camp. Weatherhead and Mr. Brevort then selected fifteen men of his party in whom he had confidence, and directed the remainder to leave. There were about fifty men of their party. I have not the least [doubt] but that they would have been murdered if these men had not been driven from their party.

They told me that anything I would ask of them would be freely given. I demanded nothing for my trouble, considering having done a good act, thereby saving the lives of two valuable citizens, was reward sufficient. However, in the Spring following they made me accept, as a present, a pair of splendid silver mounted pistols.

I returned to Rayado with Fox; turned him over to the proper authorities. He was then taken to Taos and confined, but nothing positive could be proven against him, and he was liberated.

I remained in Rayado till March and then started for St. Louis, took with me twelve wagons of Mr. Maxwell for the purpose of bringing out goods for him. Arrived at Kansas May 1. [I] proceeded to St. Louis, purchased the goods, then returned to Kansas, loaded the wagons, and started for home.

. . . I then delivered to Mr. Maxwell the wagons and goods and remained till March.

Mr. Maxwell and I rigged up a party of eighteen men to go trapping, I taking charge of them. We went to the Balla Salado, then down the South Fork to the Plains, through the Plains of Laramie to the New Park, trapped it to the Old Park, then again to the Balla Salado, then on the Arkansas where it goes out of the mountain, then followed on under the mountain, thence home to the Rayado, through to the Raton Mountain, having made a very good hunt.

I remained at Rayado during the fall and winter. In February '53, I went to the Rio Abajo and purchased sheep. Returned with them to the Rayado. Then I started for California. There was with me Henry Mercure, John Bernavette, and their employees. We had about 6,500 head of sheep. Went to Fort Laramie, then kept the wagon road that is travelled by emigrants to California, arrived about the first of August, having met with no serious loss. Sold our sheep to Mr. Norris at $5.50 a head, doing very well.

CHARLES KENNEDY (? –1871)

Although Charlie Kennedy's purported activities took place in the Moreno Valley west of Cimarron, his macabre story is included because of its sensational value to the region's folklore. The account included here is unsupported by documentation but is, nevertheless, well told.

For other versions of the sordid story, consult Agnes Morley Cleaveland's, *Satan's Paradise* (1952) and Howard Bryan's, *Robbers, Rogues and Ruffians* (1991).

A Head for Decoration

by Tom Hilton, from *Nevermore, Cimarron, Nevermore,*
Ft. Worth: Western Heritage Press, 1970, pp. 37–43

One event in the history of the Cimarron country could well be called: stranger than fiction. To tell of this we must digress for a bit. Back to the year of 1871. Back to E-Town and the Moreno Valley.

The annals of the west are filled with the deeds of killers. This too, is a story of death. One of surreptitious murder, committed under the incredible blue of high country sky and in the peaceful solitude of ancient mountains. It is also, in a way, that of buried treasure.

This is not a saga of pride shot men, facing each other with clawed hands above hardwood butt of pistol, whiskey brave and honor filled. No . . . it is an account of stealth, of men back shot or skull crushed, the sharp bite of double bit axe slicing them away from all conscious interchange. This is the story of Charles Kennedy, outcast mountain man, a drifter from lonely country to the north who in vicious evil secured for himself a place in the history of the American West. A dishonored niche, shared perhaps with the infamous Benders, those mass murderers of Kansas plains.

Charles Kennedy came into the Moreno valley of Northern New Mexico, sometime in 1865. Before those great yellow placer grounds of Elizabeth Town would begin to yield their eventual $5,000,000 and more in gold. He settled in the mouth of Fernandez Canyon at the foot of Palo Flechado Pass, that 10,000 foot high barrier on the Taos Trail. He came with a woman of Taos, her name was Rosa Villalpando. They had a son, scarcely three years of age. The woman was a virtual slave to Kennedy.

Kennedy chose his building site carefully. This part of the trail was lonely, used only by horsemen and foot travelers. The iron rimmed wheels of heavy wagons cut their ruts to the south, through Osha Pass, and down through Apache Canyon. Easier access for trail worn animals and impatient men.

A dug-out was formed against the side of the mountain, well hidden by coniferous greenery. Below the dirt rank dwelling was a spring, flowing sweet water, inviting all who passed to sojourn there. A peaceful place — but illusory — afternoon sun casting deep shadows, that sometimes hid a murderous visage, watching with mad bright eyes as greed haunted mind formulated plans for murder. Invitation to supper, but preamble to inevitable death.

It would be three years before the exodus of brain fevered men would eventually swell the population to seven thousand on the slopes above Moreno creek and begin to tear away at the earth in their endless search for gold. A time when Kennedy would see but few at the spring of death on their long journey from Taylor Crossing to Taos, and beyond. How many of these met death at the hands of the mad butcher during that time we have no way of knowing. Kennedy took that knowledge with him to the grave.

This we do know . . . soon after the rush into the placers began, rumor started to spread. Whispers, of solitary travelers seen headed for the pass, never to be seen again.

In the bitter cold winter of 1871 — a time of blue shadowed silence, over horse deep drifts — a prominent citizen of Taos rode over the rocky spine of the Sangre de Cristos, and down into Moreno Valley. He was never heard from again. Family and friends launched an investigation into his mysterious disappearance. At the shack of Kennedy, his horse and pack mules were found. Inside the smoke encrusted room his belongings were stacked in a corner. Kennedy, light hearted humor hiding deadly guilt, told the searchers that he had found the animals wandering in the canyon, and that he supposed the owner had fell victim of the Apache. The searchers knew the Indian frequented those mountains, they knew too, that the Apache favored mule meat above all things. Why then did they not kill the animals for food? But what proof of wrong doing? They rode back, not satisfied and in grave doubt. Whispers would now become growls, uttered in dimlit saloons through teeth clenched tightly over the rim of a glass containing rot gut whiskey.

Just a few weeks later a man rode up to the spring. Breaking ice to free the flow of water for man and animal, he saw, through leafless branches of aspen, the thin curl of smoke from Kennedy's cabin. He decided to investigate this evidence of human habitation. He should have drunk and fled.

There was no one about as he rode up to the filthy shack. Then, the small son of Kennedy appeared to stare with the curiosity of the isolated at the stranger. The man spoke: "Say boy, what's that smell around here? Your pappy a trapper or something"?

"No he ain't. That's the Indian papa killed the other day. He ain't had no time to chop him up and burn him yet," answered the boy with the last words he would ever speak on this earth.

Charles Kennedy had come up on the far side of the cabin

and had heard it all. He stepped into the open. The stranger saw glittering eyes in a beard covered face, madness evident. Spurs raked sorrel flanks. The horse was swift, a bullet is faster yet. One shot! Soft grey lead penetrated the softer bone of skull. Brains and face exploded redly on white snow, as the body slid lifeless from moving saddle.

Kennedy grabbed the boy by his heels, two or three swings against unyielding rock of chimney and the small head became only bloody pulp, mangled remembrance of life that had been only moments before. With a skill born of long practice, he then dismembered the bodies. In a roaring fire — aided in his work by bellows — the cremations were complete. The awful stench of burning flesh and hair, spreading slowly over peaceful surroundings.

The brute proceeded to get insanely drunk. He paid no attention to the grief stricken mother who sat silently in one dark corner. Black eyes filled with blacker hatred, watching . . . waiting. The slobbering hulk finally passed into a drunken sleep. Why the woman did not kill the sleeping beast is beyond all reason, yet she did not. It was fifteen miles over frozen, snow covered hills to Elizabeth Town. She walked it in thin moccasins.

In Herberger's saloon, the fire was hot, the whiskey hotter, and all was right in the world. Clay Allison and young Dave Crockett were there that night for some reason or other and they stared in disbelief at the half frozen apparition that burst through the heavy doors, babbling incoherently in her broken English. Enough was understood in the mad ravings to explain the many men who had disappeared on the trail. She told them: Kennedy had the bones of twenty men buried behind the cabin, that he had also killed two other of their children before coming into the valley.

Action was swift, few words needed. Hard eyed men rode off into the night, their tight faces deep behind sheepskins, protection against blade sharp wind. Predators stalked the night, in search of a predator.

Kennedy was brought back to E-Town, along with a sack of

blackened bones rattling against leather fender of saddle. Next day a trial was held — an unusual occurrence — M.W. Mills took over the defense of Kennedy. Mills was a young attorney, highly ambitious and with great political dreams. A firm conviction that always . . . the end justified the means. Somehow, someway — it is said because sweat dampened money changed hands — the jury could not reach a verdict. The killer was placed in a make shift jail for the night, to await another trial. It never came to be. That night, the men, led by Allison, came for him. Rough fibers of manila rope the last thing that inhuman butcher ever felt. The time was January 16, 1871. People could once again travel in peace over Palo Flechado.

The moon can shine with exceptional brilliance in the clear night of the high country. Thus it was that the light caught and held the blade of a long knife in Allison's hand, and sparkled in prismatic display as the first quick incision was made under the chin of the corpse. Holding the greasy hair in one hand, the blade firmly embedded in the dead flesh, he stepped around the stiffening form on the ground. One violent twist and the head came free, trailing nerve ends, blood vessels and ragged flesh that exposed neck bone. Laughing like hell, he and Dave rode east for Cimarron. Justice had been served, and the narrow confines of Cimarron Canyon echoed their self righteous pride in vigilante deed.

The few men in Lambert's Saloon and Billiard Parlor, were as one in their curiosity about the blood stained sack in Allison's grip. He stepped to the pool table and rolled its gruesome contents out for all to see, telling as he did so, the need to display the prize so that all men might know the high caliber of law and order that prevailed in the Cimarron country. Know too, the penalty for transgression. He wanted Lambert to place the head over the saloon door in a place of honor. They compromised and the bloody thing was secured to a pike pole and stuck at the southwest corner of the building. Allison was heard expressing regret that Cimarron had no taxidermist, if it had, the trophy could be "stuffed".

For over a year the sightless eyes rotted slowly in the blazing sun, the skin becoming drum tight leather. Later it was given to the Smithsonian Institute: "An abnormal specimen" they reported. For years there after, Kennedy would live on in the threats of nerve torn mothers directed at mischievous scamps, and bodiless heads were seen floating in terrified darkness from the scant protection of feather comforters. Dreams were not very pleasant then.

This now brings us to the question of treasure. That inevitable proposition ever present in any tale of the west where sudden death figured. Kennedy was said to have murdered between 15 and 100 men during his brief career. The truth lies somewhere between these two figures. He killed for gain, yet he was never able to dispose of his proceeds. Fear of discovery ever present. This during a time when fortunes were quickly dug out of the earth. When other fortunes were acquired by merchant and trader. That Kennedy gained from his murder, there can be no doubt. That he of necessity buried it, there can be no question. It is highly doubtful if any of it was ever recovered.

The rubble of his dug-out is still partially visible. Somewhere in the immediate vicinity must lie the ill gotten gains of his evil life. In some shallow hole or under a slab of sandstone, must be the disintegrating bags of nuggets and coin. Tangible evidence of the frailty of life in those days long gone. There must be a cache also, of personal items from the victims, such as spurs, guns, etc., things he had to hide. Unless of course it was all melted in his forge, or unless he told Mills about it in a vain attempt to save his wretched life. Who can say?

There are old men, and women also, who can remember tales told of this place. They say that of a night, when wind rustled a thousand leaves and moon became hidden behind scudding clouds, the screams of the dying could be heard. That the smell of burning flesh would permeate all things, and walking in search would be a body that had no head.

O.P. MCMAINS (1840-1899)

Reverend O.P. McMains came to Cimarron in 1875 as assistant to Reverend F.J. Tolby who, before his mysterious murder in Cimarron Canyon, had led the crusade for settlers' rights against the Maxwell Land Grant Company. McMains took over Tolby's campaign and championed the cause until his death. Ultimately, however, the effort failed.

In the account of McMains' activities that follows, author William Keleher inexplicably gives Tolby's initials as "T.J." instead of "F.J." Tolby's first name was Franklin. Otherwise, the account is well substantiated.

For a full biography of McMains, consult Morris F. Taylor's, *O.P. McMains and the Maxwell Land Grant Conflict* (1979).

Reverend O.P. McMains.

Ministers of the Gospel

by William A. Keleher, from *Maxwell Land Grant:
A New Mexico Item* Santa Fe: Rydal Press, 1942, pp. 75–82

>-+-+-0-+-+-<

Desperadoes, outlaws, peace officers and men who were neither outlaws nor peace officers, but just ordinary citizens, all had their troubles in the early days of the Maxwell Land Grant. Cimarron, Red River, Elizabethtown and other towns in the Grant area attracted men of all types and characters. Even clergymen were not exempt from the circumstances of the day. Soon after the close of the Civil War, Rev. Thomas Harwood, a one-man army of the Lord, arrived in northern New Mexico and spent his days and years in the service of the Methodist Episcopal Church. He and his fellow ministers preached the gospel to all who would listen, but at times few would hear or heed. There was the talk of gold discoveries on the land grant, excitement incident to acquiring land for ranches and homesteads, the turmoil that was present because of the presence of nearby Fort Union. Liquor, dance halls and gambling houses helped mightily to lure men from the atmosphere of religion.

Murder and sudden death were no novelty in the Grant area, but the murder of a minister of the gospel was something of a sensation. Rev. T.J. Tolby, a Methodist minister, who rode the circuit between Cimarron and Elizabethtown, was found murdered on September 14, 1875, at a place about twenty miles from Cimarron on the Elizabethtown road. The minister's horse was found tied to a tree some three hundred yards from his body, the saddle nine hundred yards away in another direction. Robbery was not the motive because Rev. Tolby's personal effects were intact, his horse, saddle and outfit not stolen.

Immediately following the discovery of the body, anti-grant men charged the murder to Grant men, because the minister had on numerous occasions strongly expressed the view that the Grant belonged to the Indians. He had even gone so far as to begin negotiations for the purchase of a large tract of land along the Vermejo, in Colfax County, as the first step in a program to help rehabilitate the Utes and Apaches.

Governor S.B. Axtell, of the Territory of New Mexico, offered a reward of $500.00 for the apprehension and conviction "of the perpetrator of the dreadful crime of the murder of Rev. T.J. Tolby," but the reward was never claimed. The murderer was never apprehended. Buried with honors of the Masonic Lodge in Cimarron, eulogized by a young lawyer, Frank W. Springer, later to become famous in the Maxwell Land Grant fight on the side of the owners, the murder of Rev. Mr. Tolby continued to be the subject of penetrating inquiry. Rev. O.P. McMains, a fellow minister of the gospel, was greatly affected by Rev. Mr. Tolby's death. He dropped his work for a time as a preacher and turned detective. From clues obtained, McMains was confident that Cruz Vega had killed Tolby. McMains' suspicions enmeshed him in a chain of situations which brought him to trial for murder, caused the sudden death of three men and precipitated much trouble for the church with which he was affiliated.

On October 1, 1875, two weeks and a day after Tolby had been found murdered, the body of Cruz Vega was found hanging to a telegraph pole, about three quarters of a mile north of the Ponil River, in Colfax County, about a mile and a half north of Cimarron. The taut lariat about the neck of Cruz Vega told the story grimly enough. He had been lynched and had been badly treated before being strung up. Bunches of hair had been torn from his scalp and he had been tortured in other ways.

Bit by bit the story of the lynching of Cruz Vega came to light and the Rev. O.P. McMains was pointed out as the man principally responsible for his death. McMains was arrested for the murder of Cruz Vega, tried before a jury in Mora County District Court on a change of venue from Colfax County, on August 23 and 24, 1877. Col. William Breeden, Attorney-General for the Territory, prosecuted the case for the people, and Frank Springer of Cimarron and Judge William D. Lee of the Vermejo, represented the defendant. The jury was composed of Pedro Morris, Juan

Ortega, Benjamin Loewenstein, Concepcion Trujillo, Noverto Saavedra, Nestor Maes, Sacramento Cashmore, Jose Maes Carenias, George W. Scroggins, George Cashmore, Candelaria Bustes and Julian Solis. McMains was found guilty "in the fifth degree," and fined three hundred dollars. Henry L. Waldo, the trial judge, set aside the verdict, which read: "We, the jury find the defendant guilty in the fifth degree and assess the penalty at three hundred dollars." Judge Waldo held that the verdict did not say of what the defendant had been found guilty. McMains was to go to trial again, but the case was dismissed at Taos by Judge Samuel Parks on April 1, 1878. The *Las Vegas Gazette*, in commenting on the case in its issue of April 6, 1878, said:

"The case against Rev. O.P. McMains for the murder of Cruz Vega was dismissed at Taos by Judge Samuel Parks. The Legislature repealed the law attaching Colfax to Taos County for judicial purposes, and under which law the indictment was found. This rendered the indictment null and void and consequently the case was easily disposed of. The true situation is that under the evidence McMains could not properly be convicted of murder. The instructions of Judge Waldo at Mora were a virtual acquittal."

Testimony at the trial of McMains at Mora developed many interesting facts. Isaiah Rinehart testified that McMains had asked him to induce Cruz Vega to meet McMains and answer questions that he proposed to ask him in connection with the death of Tolby. McMains had told Rinehart, he testified, that he had interviewed "all the people and they were certain that Vega was implicated in the murder of Rev. Tolby." Rinehart was either unwilling or unable to arrange for the interview, but William Low, a resident in the Moreno Valley, succeeded in employing Cruz Vega to watch his corn fields at night, using that as a pretext for an interview by McMains. By prearrangement, a lighted bonfire in Low's corn field was to be a signal for a group of men to gather. McMains had the idea, so Rinehart testified, that if he and a crowd of men showing force could interview Vega, they could get him to confess to the murder of Tolby, or tell who had killed him. At the signal of the lighted bonfire, a group of men gathered, with McMains present to do the interrogating. McMains attempted to direct the men in their work, but the crowd got out of hand, began to make short work of Vega and finally lynched him.

McMains remained at Low's house during the night, and got up crying, showing signs of great distress. "What is the matter now, Mr. McMains?" was Low's testimony. "Did you hear that shooting last night?" asked McMains. "I came away last night when I found out that I had no control over those men," continued McMains.

The men in the lynching party were all disguised, according to Low, and McMains was wearing a disguise, but disclosed his identity when one of the men in the crowd asked him to step forward.

Cruz Vega at the interview, before being lynched, denied all responsibility for the murder of Tolby, but declared that a man named Manuel Cardenas might know something about it, and that was all he could tell them.

The mere mention by Cruz Vega of the name Manuel Cardenas proved an unfortunate circumstance for that gentleman. The "Vigilantes," as they called themselves, waited patiently until November 10, 1875, for the return of Manuel Cardenas. The mob waylaid him, shot him to death. No public sympathy was forthcoming when Cardenas was assassinated. Newspapers of the day explained that "Cardenas had a bad reputation; that at one time he had been sentenced for murder, and only a short time before he was killed, had been publicly whipped in the Plaza of Taos."

The lynching of Cruz Vega, however, was a different matter. Vega was well known in the community of Cimarron, was serving as a constable of Cimarron precinct at the time of his death. On November 1, 1875, Francisco Griego, commonly called "Pancho," made strong threats against certain people in Cimarron because of the lynching of Vega, to whom he had been related. Griego talked and made threats in the presence of R.C. (Clay) Allison at the St. James Hotel. Allison had nothing whatever to do with the Vega lynching, but promptly shot and killed Griego, when the latter insisted, as Allison claimed, on quarreling with him. Allison had shot two bullets in killing Griego, then ran everybody out of the bar of the St. James Hotel. The bar was locked up and Griego's body was not released to relatives until the next day. The shooting of Griego by Allison in Cimarron was merely a passing incident in the life of R. "Clay" Allison. Nothing was done to him because of the death of "Pancho" Griego.

During the Civil War Clay Allison had gone into the Confederate Army in Tennessee as a boy and a private, and had come out a man and an officer, tradition says, a captain. Whether private or captain, Clay Allison was destined to carve for himself, not only notches in his gun in New Mexico and southern Colorado, but a place in the affairs of Southwestern gunmen. Clay Allison, accompanied by his brother, John Allison, trailed a large number of cattle from the Texas Panhandle, where they had gone after leaving Tennessee, into the attractive grass-land country of Colfax County, New Mexico.

The Allison brothers had never heard of the Maxwell Land Grant, of Miranda and Beaubien, or Lucien B. Maxwell. They saw a mighty country, with rivers racing down from mountain sides, with springs gushing abundant water from high hills. They saw grass that reminded them of the grass that grew on the hill sides of their native Tennessee. Here was a country worth while at long last. The Allison brothers camped on the Maxwell Grant at a place of their choice, called it a ranch, turned their cattle out to graze, and woe to those who questioned their rights or asked to see leases or titles. "Grant-men," so-called because they were in opposition to those claiming to own and control the Maxwell Land Grant, were quick to recognize in the Allisons men who were lightning-fast on the draw, who had the voice of authority, the courage to back up a command. Clay Allison enjoyed the atmosphere of Cimarron. The town was wide open, there was plenty of hard liquor and plenty of action. Clay Allison liked liquor, craved action. Brother John Allison was quiet, unassuming, but had the reputation of being a cooler man, and a better shot than Clay. Although John Allison disliked to pick a quarrel, he would stick to the end to see a fight through. The Allisons played a lone hand in the cattle business. They were capable cowmen and their neighbors respected them.

On December 30, 1876, Clay Allison and John Allison went from Cimarron to Las Animas, Colorado, and attended a dance in the Olympic dance hall. Town Marshal Chas. Feber learned of their presence in Las Animas, immediately went to the dance hall and asked them to surrender their guns for the evening. The Allisons politely refused. Feber went out of the hall and soon returned with a shotgun. In the gunplay that followed, both Allisons fired at the same instant. Marshal Feber fell, mortally wounded, but as he was dying, pulled the trigger of his shotgun, wounding John Allison. The Allisons continued to fire bullets into the lifeless body of Marshal Feber. As Clay went over to the slumping body of his brother, he dragged Feber's body with him, and cried out: "John here's the man who shot you. Look at the damned son of a bitch. I killed him." Sheriff Spiers and a posse arrested the Allison brothers shortly after the shooting. Clay assumed all the blame, but claimed he shot in self-defense. The grand jury convened on March 31, 1877, but refused to indict him, and Clay Allison returned to his ranch in Colfax County near the town of Otero. The Santa Fe *New Mexican* of December 8, 1878, described Clay Allison as a "half breed Indian," and claimed that during the Civil War he was a leader of bushwhackers in Tennessee, "where he plundered union and rebel alike."

Rev. O.P. McMains, finally free from the difficulties that had surrounded him because of his zeal in attempting to ferret out the murderer of his late Brother Tolby, returned to his affiliation with "anti-grant" men on the Maxwell Land Grant. McMains was one of the most fearless, persistent and relentless fighters on the side of the anti-grant men. He carried his fight from protest meetings in New Mexico to the Congress of the United States. By nature a crusader and an intense partisan, McMains took over the fight against the Grant owners as an agent for settlers and squatters, was elected to the New Mexico Legislature. He had settled on some land of the Grant himself and was personally interested in defeating the claims of the Grant company. At last, however, after litigation that lasted for years, McMains was ejected through court decree from his ranch on the Grant. The Sheriff of Colfax County, with execution in hand, gathered up McMains' horses and cattle to satisfy a judgment for costs of the litigation and in connection with the eviction. The Sheriff advertised the livestock for sale. On the day of the sale, fifty ranchers and cowboys attended, formed a ring around the livestock, cocked their revolvers and held their rifles loosely across the pommels of saddles. The leader of the cowboys told the Sheriff, crying the sale, that they were going to kill the first man who made an offer. No offers being made, a cowboy stepped forward, gun in hand, opened the corral gate where the livestock had been impounded for the sale, and turned them out on the open range. The cowboys then gathered the cattle and horses together, restored them to friends of McMains, who kept them for him. McMains was finally obliged to leave the premises involved in the ejectment suit, and found out, as the Indians and Spanish-Americans had found out before him, that he had no ownership of any part of the Maxwell Land Grant.

The McMains' execution sale was the culmination of the war he had carried on against the Grant people for many years. McMains had openly charged that the Secretary of the Interior, John W. Noble, had "wrongfully refused to enforce the valid order of the Department of the Interior of January 28, 1874, requiring lands claimed by The Maxwell Land Grant claimants to be treated as public lands," and claimed that "this wrongful procedure of the Secretary of the Interior," was in the interest of a conspiracy in 1877, of Hon. S.B. Elkins, then a delegate in Congress from New Mexico, and of Hon. T.B. Catron, then United States Attorney for New Mexico, and Hon. J.A. Williamson, then Commissioner of the General Land Office, "to defeat the enforcement of said valid order of January 28, 1874, and to deprive homestead and preemption settlers of private and vested rights, without due process of law, and to defraud the United States of its surveyed land by prosecuting anew the adjudicated Maxwell Claim against the United States in violation of Section 5498 of the Revised

Statutes." McMains in an affidavit filed with the Committee on Public Lands on May 9, 1892, claimed that the Secretary of the Interior and the Commissioner of Public Lands were "aiding and abetting by trick and fraud," the conspiracy of Elkins, Catron and Williamson, and "were shielding them, as far as in them lies, the aforesaid conspirators, from the punishment at least of exposure and consequent dishonor and disgrace."

CLAY ALLISON (1841–1887)

Clay Allison was one of those types frequently encountered in the American West—a bad, good guy, who seemed always to be on hand when trouble erupted. Folklore and history has it that, fueled by whiskey from the St. James Hotel, Allison periodically participated in shootings either in the saloon or out in the street and always in an effort to right some wrong.

Numerous short accounts of Allison's life have been written, both while he was in the Cimarron country and other places in New Mexico and Texas. Interested readers may wish to consult Chuck Parsons's biography *Clay Allison, Portrait of a Shootist* (1983) or John Truett's historical novel *Clay Allison: Legend of Cimarron* (1998).

Clay Allison

Clay Allison's Cimarron

by Norman Cleaveland, *New Mexico Magazine*
Vol. 52, Nos. 3-4, March/April 1974, pp. 11-15, 38-48

Clay Allison earned his greatest fame as a corpse-maker in Cimarron, then the county seat of Colfax County in northeastern New Mexico. In the 1870s, Allison became a legend in his own time.

Legends about Clay emanated both from devoted friends and implacable enemies. They were gradually embellished by narrators of those tall tales that were a major source of frontier entertainment. It's only natural that Clay's true character remains shrouded in the mists of controversy.

One thing seems certain: a historical judgement of Allison based on the true character of his most powerful foes makes him a hero in New Mexico.

My grandfather, William Raymond Morley, was an executive of the Maxwell Land Grant and Railway Company, with headquarters in Cimarron. For a time, Clay considered Morley to be an enemy because:

Morley had marched with General Sherman of the Union Army of the Tennessee, while Allison had ridden with General Nathan Bedford Forrest of the Confederate Army of the Tennessee.

The Maxwell Land Grant was illegal and unjust. Though its owners put it at almost two million acres, there were legal arguments that it was only about 97,000 acres. The Maxwell company sought to collect rents from ranchers and miners whom it considered squatters.

The Maxwell company and local officials were manipulated by the Santa Fe Ring, a clique that had dominated New Mexico's political and economic life from about 1868.

The life expectancy of enemies of either Allison or the Ring was short. When Morley was on the hate lists of both, it is little short of a miracle that he survived.

A common foe—the Ring—eventually caused Allison to forgive Morley's Civil War role and become an ally . . . which almost certainly prolonged Morley's life.

Grandfather Morley, born in Massachusetts in 1846, had been orphaned early and raised by an uncle in Iowa. After the Civil War, he studied two years at Iowa State University, then went to work as a civil engineer on westward-expanding railroads. In 1871, he joined the Maxwell company, the next year becoming its executive vice president.

In 1872, Morley persuaded Frank Springer, a brilliant classmate, to come to New Mexico. Springer was a lawyer. Morley needed legal talent to cope with the complexities of managing the Maxwell company, with its British and Dutch fiscal entanglements. In time, Morley also needed Springer's expertise to cope with the abundance of legal talent in the Santa Fe Ring.

The next year, Morley married and brought to Cimarron 21-year-old Ada McPherson, his golden-haired childhood sweetheart. As a fringe benefit of his job, they occupied part of a luxurious 40-room adobe mansion built by Lucien Bonaparte Maxwell, former owner of the grant. My grandmother Ada, an accomplished pianist, played for many a Cimarron social event.

Allison's admirers maintain he never killed anyone who didn't need killing. It should be emphasized that Clay was primarily a rancher, a particularly competent one. He was just as competent with six-shooter and bowie knife. This competence he was willing to demonstrate even when justice for himself was not involved. As rancher George Coe put it, "When Allison butted in, business started to pick up." (Coe was to become a figure in the Lincoln County War that boosted young Billy the Kid to fame.) The late Southwestern literateur J. Frank Dobie described Clay as "Don Quixote of the Six-Shooter." Perhaps "Ombudsman with a Six-Shooter" would be even more appropriate.

In his ably researched *The Gunfighters*, Dale T. Schoenberger concludes that Allison "suffered from manic-depressive psychosis." Many another crusader—John Brown, Johnny Appleseed, Billy Mitchell—has been called mad.

Addiction to liquor increased Clay's mental instability. When in his cups, he would bring Cimarron business to a full stop, all doors locked, all streets deserted. Drunk or sober, though he commanded respect.

While not a regular churchgoer, Clay himself had much respect for religion. And, drunk or sober, he was inclined to the robust singing of hymns. There's an apparently valid story that, summoning a reluctant clergyman, he interrupted roistering one Christmas eve in a Cimarron saloon with a demand for a full church service. With Clay's six-shooter much in evidence, all present reverently took part.

Next to liquor, dancing was Allison's favorite hobby. He was addicted to the fandango, a lively Spanish dance. His presence enlivened many a Cimarron social gathering.

With women present, Clay's manners accorded with the best tradition of Southern gallantry. This appeal was augmented by a lithe six-foot-two figure, wavy brown hair, handsome features and striking blue eyes that were ever so slightly cocked. A sparkling sense of humor added to his popularity among the women . . . all of them, that is, except mothers of marriageable daughters.

Among the latter was Scotland-born Mrs. Robina Crawford Bishop, yesterday's "hostess with the mostest" along the Santa Fe Trail. When her family emigrated to Wisconsin, she married Bishop, who worked his way west in railroad construction. Meantime, she bore "the three prettiest girls on the frontier," in the opinion of future Territorial Governor Miguel A. Otero.

The vivacious but diminutive Mrs. Bishop tried to teach the lanky Clay the Highland fling—which in itself must have been an eyeful—but Clay's eyes were on her second daughter Josephine. Clay was not what Mrs. Bishop had in mind for a son-in-law. When Clay came a-courtin' Josephine one evening, Mrs. Bishop took up a broom and chased him out of the house.

Clay feigned great indignation. Common decency, he proclaimed far and wide, demanded that nothing less imposing than a shotgun should have been used to get rid of a man of his reputation . . . particularly when the aggressor was a woman and not quite five feet tall.

At his ranch some 10 miles north of Cimarron, Clay saw to it that at least one cowhand could play the fiddle. At his ranch house and around campfires, there often would be dancing. If his wearied hands proved reluctant, Clay would dance solo.

Dancing stopped abruptly when injustice demanded attention. In Clay's eyes, as well as those of many others, injustice was becoming rampant in Colfax County. Blamed were both the Maxwell company and the Santa Fe Ring.

The Ring's key figure was Stephen B. (Smooth Steve) Elkins, who in 1873 became New Mexico's territorial delegate to Congress. Close to Elkins was Thomas B. Catron, the U.S. attorney. Both Elkins and Catron were lawyers from Missouri.

Elkins proved to be one of the most accomplished politicians in Washington, eventually becoming a secretary of war and a senator from West Virginia. Elkins teamed with one of the nation's most potent lobbyists, Collis P. Huntington of the Southern Pacific Railroad. Huntington sought a monopoly in New Mexico to match the railroad's in California. Samuel B. Axtell, who was appointed New Mexico's governor in 1875, had come from California, where he served Huntington well. Thus, the Ring was firmly entrenched in Washington as well as in Santa Fe.

The Ring's political control extended from successive territorial governors down to town constables. *Pistoleros* were handy when bought officials and corrupted courts needed support.

A neat arrangement of New Mexico's courts simplified matters for the Ring. Justices of the State Supreme Court also served as judges of the district courts. They handled appeals against their own decisions. Thus, one Joseph G. Palen not only sat as chief justice but also was district judge for the Colfax area.

The Ring's judges adopted a common means of harassing uncooperative persons living some distance from the seat of a court. This was to have a summons served on such a person for some frivolous reason. Upon the accused's appearance, the judge repeatedly would delay a hearing. This caused much expense and inconvenience.

Among Colfax Country ranchers so inconvenienced were George Coe—whom you've already met—and several Coe relatives. The Coes had settled in the Sugarite Valley, some 50 miles northeast of Cimarron. They were charged with trespassing by a cattleman who had leased the Sugarite from the Maxwell company.

After their hearing before Judge Palen in Cimarron had been postponed one week for a third time, Allison "butted in," to use George Coe's term. Clay let it be known that the situation was "graveling" him. This was a clear indication, again to cite Coe, that business was about to pick up.

Allison told the plaintiff to move on, the farther the better. Then Clay called on Judge Palen with word that he was now acting as the Coe's special attorney. He "urged" that there be no further delays to a hearing.

Allison made no apology for neglecting to remove his six-shooter before entering Palen's chambers. An indignant Palen said he had a good notion to charge Clay with contempt of court. For whatever reason, he didn't.

At a hearing next day, the plaintiff failed to appear. The charges against the Coes were dismissed.

Such a bold challenge to legal authority added many hardy ranchers to Clay's devoted backers. With such support, he became an ever sharper thorn to the Santa Fe Ring.

Morley clearly comprehended the Ring's land policy: ". . . to divide the people by getting some to lease all the ranges at a nominal price and try to drive others off by . . . [getting] up a feud . . ." As for his own policy toward "squatters," he was "claiming that they [the Maxwell company] are entitled to rent but making no fuss about it on account of the question of unsettled title."

From Morley's arrival in Cimarron, he had operated a weekly paper for the Maxwell company. In late 1874, he and Frank Springer bought what became the Cimarron *News and Press* and hired one Will Dawson as an editor-printer. "It promises to be connected with the [Maxwell] corporation and independent in politics," they pledged. Within 14 months the *News and Press* could boast a circulation "second to none in the Territory," largely because it was one of the few papers not dominated by the Santa Fe Ring.

In June 1875, Francisco (Pancho) Griego, a deputy sheriff and foreman of the Colfax County grand jury, was dealing monte, a gambling card game, at his usual stand in the St. James Hotel's saloon. Three soldiers from Ft. Union, some 50 miles south, were on hand. Griego got into a row with them. They ran from the saloon. Griego shot at all three, killing two and wounding one. It turned out that all three soldiers had been unarmed.

Reported the *News and Press*:

. . . the military now assert that he [Griego] has killed two or three soldiers before in gambling rows. He is well known throughout the county, and it seems hardly probable but that sooner or later he will be . . . tried before a legal tribunal for his part in the bloody affair.

All this probably lost Griego his job as deputy sheriff and grand jury foreman, but Pancho retained sufficient political influence in Santa Fe to obtain an amnesty. Of equal importance to the Ring probably was Griego's reputation as a *pistolero*, one perhaps surpassed only by Clay Allison's in Colfax County.

That same spring of 1875, Mrs. Morley's mother, Mary Tibbles McPherson, came from Iowa to visit the family and see for the first time the Morley's daughter Agnes, born the year before.

Mrs. McPherson's late attorney-husband Marcus had been an Iowa politico who crusaded for women's property rights. A brother Thomas was a Methodist minister and Nebraska editor; he and his wife Bright Eyes, daughter of a Ponca chief, crusaded for Indian rights. With such a background, it was instinctive for Mrs. McPherson to react to the skullduggery seen all about her in New Mexico . . . and to do some crusading herself.

Mrs. McPherson wrote a scathing letter to Washington, probably either to the secretary of the interior or to the attorney general. She dropped it into an uncovered wooden receiving box at the postoffice.

Daughter Ada learned of this. She felt the Morleys were having troubles enough without her mother's getting into the act. In full view of Mrs. Bishop and others, she retrieved the letter from the box. (One of Mrs. Bishop's daughters had married John McCullough, who was the Cimarron postmaster. Mrs. Bishop helped her son-in-law.)

The story of the letter's retrieval quickly made the Cimarron rounds. Two Santa Fe Ring henchmen, Dr. R.H. Longwill, the probate judge, and Melvin W. Mills, a member of the Territorial Legislature, heard it. Postmaster McCullough had no recourse but to report the incident. This brought U.S. Attorney Catron into the matter. The Ring was alert for any chance to strike at the increasingly antagonistic Morley.

In July 1875, Ada made a buckboard round trip of some 300 miles to Santa Fe with plaintiff McCullough and witness Mrs. Bishop. She was indicted by a federal grand jury for robbing the mails. Later, a warrant was issued for her arrest.

Though Clay Allison still considered Morley an enemy, he found it intolerable that a woman, even a Yankee woman, be prosecuted — persecuted, that is — to harass her husband. Clay again butted in. He issued an edict, probably in a crowded Cimarron saloon, that "if Mrs. Morley is ever brought to trial, not a man will leave the courtroom alive."

The arrest warrant was never served.

Therein lies another story. Both of the Morleys actually seemed eager to have a trial proceed. In fact, grandfather eventually wrote U.S. Attorney General Alphonso Taft (whose son would become President) to that effect. But Catron was having second thoughts. It is presumed he feared the letter's becoming part of the public record. It would have provided much unwelcome evidence against the Santa Fe Ring.

Living in Cimarron was the Rev. T.J. Tolby, a Methodist circuit rider. Tolby was crusading to have the bulk of the Maxwell Land Grant bought by the U.S. government and turned over to the

Utes and Apaches, as Kit Carson had advocated earlier. Tolby also shared the mounting indignation over the Santa Fe Ring. And he was publicly appalled by the amnesty granted Griego.

Both Mrs. Morley and her mother, devout Methodists, admired Tolby. Morley himself, while not a Methodist, cooperated with Tolby in *News and Press* attacks on the Ring. What's more, they were jointly credited, perhaps, erroneously, with writing a series of letters to the New York *Sun* about conditions in New Mexico. Publication of these displeased Elkins, Catron and other Ring members.

In September 1875, Tolby was met on a Cimarron street by Chief Justice Palen. In the presence of bystanders, Palen denounced the minister for remarks he had made about his court. Tolby defiantly replied, Springer was to depose later, that he would "write up the judge so that 200,000 readers should see the record."

On September 14, Tolby conducted services at Elizabethtown, some 35 miles west. Two days later, his body was found, a bullet in the back, in Cimarron Canyon. There was no evidence of robbery.

This caused an uproar in Colfax County, including the Allison contingent. Clay's respect for religion extended to its clerics, especially to the crusading Tolby.

Clay limited his initial concern to Tolby's widow and two small daughters. He promptly raised enough money to send them back to Indiana. Clay was an ingenious fund-raiser for causes he considered worthy, as was soon to become evident.

The duly-constituted authorities seemed reluctant to question even the most obvious suspects. For instance, Pancho Griego's nephew Cruz Vega had been in the vicinity of the murder site during a one-day stint as a substitute mail carrier. Fresh in the minds of Tolby's friends was Griego's own immunity to the law. Had his nephew also acquired a license to kill?

And certainly the threats of New Mexico's chief justice supported a grave suspicion that the Santa Fe Ring was involved.

Allison's patience became exhausted after six full weeks of inaction. He butted in, leading a mob that not only questioned

Vega, who implicated one Manuel Cardenas, but finally lynched him.

At Vega's funeral, Griego publicly vowed to kill Allison on sight. News of Pancho's challenge brought Clay on a brisk trot from his ranch. He knew he would find Griego at the St. James saloon. Of many versions as to what ensued, the late Fred Lambert, son of the hotel's French-born proprietor Henri, told me his father had witnessed the following:

Saintt James Hotel during the Colfax County War.

Arriving after dark, Clay met Griego at the door and said, "I understand you're looking for me."

"Yes," replied Griego.

"What do you want?"

"Let's have a drink first."

Griego agreed. They did so. Glasses replaced on the bar, both went for their guns. Allison's first shot hit Griego in the forehead. As Griego fell, Clay put two more bullets into him. Then he shot out the barroom lights.

The Colfax County War was on!

Griego's body was not removed until morning. Allison came in for some criticism because Griego's horse remained saddled and tied to the hitching rack all night—not good enough for a cowboy and particularly not worthy of a former cavalryman.

On the other hand, ex-Confederate Allison had unwittingly avenged the murders of several federal troopers. This probably earned him much respect at Ft. Union.

Cardenas, the man fingered by Vega, told a justice of the peace in Elizabethtown that Vega had killed Tolby. Cardenas did add that Longwill and Mills had offered him $500 to do the job.

When word of this reached Cimarron, Longwill took off for Ft. Union with Allison in hot pursuit. Longwill got there just in time. He came under military protection at the dictates of the Ring's Governor Axtell. Later, he went on to Santa Fe and out of the scene.

Mills, arriving at Cimarron by stage from a business trip to Colorado, faced a lynch mob, but cooler heads prevailed. A detachment ordered from Ft. Union by the governor took Mills into custody.

At a justice of the peace trial in mid-November 1875, Mills was dismissed for lack of evidence, while Cardenas was found guilty as an accessory. Led back to jail, Cardenas was killed by a shot in the night. His assassin was never identified.

In a desperate effort to restore its control in Colfax County, the Ring now, in January 1876, had a submissive Territory Legislature attach Colfax to Taos County for judicial purposes. The Tolby investigation would be further stymied. The aroused Colfax citizenry would be bypassed for jury duty. As Morley later put it, the Ring was taking this means "to punish Colfax County for presuming to interfere in such matters."

The Ring's leadership was determined to indict Clay Allison and destroy his leadership of the Colfax County cattlemen and townspeople. This was a Ring retaliation for the killing of Vega, Griego and Cardenas and the effort to involve Longwill and Mills in the Tolby murder.

With the outbreak of the Colfax County War, the Maxwell company's affairs became so involved that Morley and Springer sought to cut their workload by turning over editorial duties entirely to Dawson. Dawson apparently unable to resist the Ring's blandishments, promptly reversed *News and Press* policy. Becoming ever bolder, Dawson referred unkindly to Clay Allison.

On January 19, 1876, Clay and some of his cohorts registered their displeasure by blowing up the weekly's press (black gunpowder being readily at hand) and throwing its remnants into the close-by Cimarron River.

In his cups, Clay then picked up an armful of a partially printed edition and made the rounds of Cimarron selling the issues as "the Clay Allison Extra." He charged whatever he thought a customer could afford. None dared haggle or refuse to buy. Bishop was one of many indignant citizens who paid $1.

Morley had long maintained a reliable early-warning service of Clay's rampages. He was not to be found that night.

Next morning, Clay met grandmother standing at the scene of destruction. She raked him over the coals, for the loss of the press was a financial blow.

For once set back on his heels, Clay apologized profusely and handed Ada Morley a roll of greenbacks (variously reported from $200 to $600), probably proceeds from sale of "the Clay Allison Extra." "I don't fight women," he said abashedly. "Go buy yourself another press."

(Actually, the Morleys took parts from an older press in the shop and cannibalized some from the smashed press to get back into publication promptly.)

Of even more significance in the Clay-Ada confrontation, Allison assured Mrs. Morley that henceforth the Morleys would receive his wholehearted support. This was a major shift in the Colfax County power structure.

As for editor Dawson, he speedily disappeared from the scene.

Morley family financial woes that grandmother had professed to Clay were real indeed. Maxwell had sold the grant for

$750,000. British and Dutch stockholders put up $5 million to take it over. Ring policies were milking the investment. Catron was on the verge of acquiring the grant for $20,000 in delinquent taxes. Only a last-minute effort by grandfather, including a personal payment of some $1,500 had saved the grant for the stockholders and from Catron and the Ring.

In February 1876, Springer, at the request of Morley and other prominent Cimarron citizens, went to Santa Fe to ask Governor Axtell to annul — as he legally could — the court site bill. Axtell was "very bitter in his allusions to the people of Colfax county," Springer deposed later, "and especially in his allusions to one R.C. [Clay] Allison, whom he denounce as a murderer . . . and declared he was going to have him indicted and punished and compel him to leave the country."

Returning to Cimarron, the group drafted a formal invitation to the governor to come there to discuss the courts and other troublesome matters. Signers included Allison. In a subsequent affidavit, Springer explained he had prevailed on Clay to sign because this would guarantee the governor the utmost courtesy and hospitality, "since Allison was a stickler about such things."

About mid-March, word was received that the governor would indeed visit Cimarron. He wanted to be met only by a small "welcoming committee" that specifically included Morley, Springer and Allison.

At the same time, Ben Stevens of Albuquerque was sent to Cimarron to act as district attorney of Colfax County. Stevens would have at his orders a cavalry troop to be sent from Ft. Union, under Captain Francis Moore, as the governor's escort.

Stevens received a secret "Dear Ben" letter from Axtell: ". . . Have your men placed to arrest him [Allison] and to kill all the men who resist you or stand with those who do resist you [Morley and Springer] . . . do not hesitate at extreme measures. . . ."

While Stevens owed his job to the Santa Fe Ring, assassination was too much. Stevens was on cordial terms with Morley. Thus Morley "became aware" of Axtell's letter, as he said later in an affidavit. He promptly warned Springer and Allison.

The governor was not on the designated stage. There was no one in Cimarron for the cavalry troop to escort nor was there anyone readily at hand to arrest or shoot.

It is highly probable that Captain Moore also "became aware" of the governor's instructions. He merely went through gestures of compliance. The troop rode out to Allison's ranch. Moore's offer to escort Allison back to Cimarron apparently was readily accepted. After a couple of hours in Moore's Cimarron headquarters, Allison returned to his ranch—not having been disarmed, much less arrested. As between a corrupt politician and a first-class fighting ex-cavalryman, there can be little doubt where the captain's sympathies lay.

Henry L. Waldo, an Elkins-Catron law partner also from Missouri, became chief justice when Palen died in December. Shortly, Waldo called a grand jury into being in Taos.

In a charge to it, Waldo said: "Since the beginning of the year 1875, at least 16 or 18 men have come to their deaths in brawls or by assassination, to say nothing of numerous shootings and woundings." Such had been the ferocity of the Colfax County war!

About the Tolby murder, Waldo said, "The matter should be sifted to the bottom and the guilty planners and perpetrators of this diabolic crime be brought to the bar of justice."

The jury called some 50 witnesses from Colfax County. One way, this was a trip of 55 miles over 9,102-foot Palo Flechado Pass. Besides the time and expense this meant for witnesses, the pass often was deep in snow.

In a most curious legal procedure, Attorney General William Breeden, another Ring leader, sat with the jury to "assist" in its investigation. To no one's surprise, the jury found that it "was unable to discover the least evidence" against Longwill and Mills.

Sometime during this period, Governor Axtell arranged to meet Allison aboard a stage at Vermejo, just north of Cimarron. Axtell and Allison spent the entire day together en route to Trinidad, Colorado.

Shortly, Clay was in Taos to face indictments for first-degree murder in the deaths of Chunk Colbert, a gunman he had outdrawn in 1874; Charles Cooper, a friend of Colbert who had mysteriously disappeared, and Francisco Griego. Clay was defended by Frank Springer.

The prosecutor could produce no witnesses to the Colbert killing. He couldn't produce evidence that Cooper was dead, much less that Allison had killed him. Luis Griego, Francisco's son, testified that Clay had shot his father in the back during their saloon showdown.

The jury refused to return any indictments.

What agreement had Axtell and Allison come to in that stagecoach? History gives us no answer. Clay continued to battle the Santa Fe Ring.

In October 1876, Springer married Josephine Bishop, whose hand Allison had sought. By now, the Colfax County War had made Springer and Allison firm friends, with great mutual respect. Previous bitterness over the Maxwell company and destruction of the printing press was disregarded. And the dollar that Clay had extracted from Josephine's father for "the Clay Allison Extra" apparently was considered adequate compensation for her mother's unmannerly use of a broom instead of a shotgun when chasing Clay out of her house.

The Morley-Springer-Allison Axis soon had the Santa Fe Ring in deep trouble because of Morley's mother-in-law. Mrs. McPherson became an unrelenting fury after her daughter's indictment for post office robbery. In Washington, she undertook a year-long, one-woman crusade against the Ring, to the embarrassment of Elkins and Huntington.

Finally, the big break came. In February 1878, John Henry Tunstall, an English merchant-rancher, was gunned down by a Ring-instigated posse in Lincoln County of south-central New Mexico. This signaled the outbreak of the Lincoln County War. It also brought the British Embassy into the picture, raising awkward questions about the propriety of duly-constituted American authorities murdering an unresisting British subject and leaving his body where it fell.

Finally, Frank Springer's father, Judge Francis Springer of

Iowa, exploited potent political connections in Washington — including a talk with President Hayes.

From all this pressure, Secretary of the Interior Carl Schurz in July 1878 sent Frank Warner Angel of New York, a perceptive and energetic investigator, to dig into Tunstall's murder and other violence in New Mexico.

The Ring was rude and balky, but Springer produced many affidavits for Angel testifying to its corruption. Springer also wrote one himself testifying to Clay's character: ". . . a man of Southern birth and education, of sensitive feelings and strong passions, quick to resent any indignities and a man of well-known personal courage and determination."

Angel's report was devastating. The "Dear Ben" letter was quoted in full with Angel's comment: ". . . was there ever a cooler devised plot with a Governor as sponsor?"

As for the Ring:

It is seldom that history states more corruption, fraud, mismanagement, plots and murders than New Mexico has been the theater of under the administration of Governor Axtell.

President Hayes promptly replaced Axtell with the distinguished General Lew Wallace, who had been sponsored by Judge Springer. (Wallace was to finish writing *Ben-Hur* while in Santa Fe.)

Breeden, the attorney general resigned, as did U.S. Attorney Catron.

The Colfax County War was over.

Headlined the Cimarron *News and Press*: AXTELL'S HEAD FALLS AT LAST . . . FIFTY GUNS FIRED IN HONOR OF EVENT. Upon hearing the news in Tucson, Arizona, Grandfather Morley, who had left the Maxwell company to return to railroading, wrote Ada: "I just wanted to go out in the street and throw up my hat and howl, but being a stranger it would not look well. . . . Darling, we are completely vindicated, and when I say we, I mean all who have so long struggled against this terrible ring."

Morley was to die of accidental gunshot at 36 while

surveying a rail line in Mexico. What irony after having survived the Civil War and years among the *pistoleros!*

Grandmother took her family, which had grown to three children, to west-central New Mexico and what was to become — another irony — Catron County. She became a successful rancher. Daughter Agnes was to become my mother and a New Mexico literary figure for her *No Life for a Lady* and *Satan's Paradise.*

Springer eventually abandoned law and, through much research and writing in scholarly publications, became a world-famous paleontologist.

As for another of those who "so long struggled" against the Ring, one who was a boy in Cimarron at the time provides an epitaph. In December 1935, George Crocker wrote George Fitzpatrick, former *New Mexico* editor, that "Colfax County should erect a monument in honor of Clay Allison for hunting down the Tolby murderers."

MANLY M. CHASE (1842–1915)

In 1870 Manly Chase traded a herd of wild horses to Lucien Maxwell for a thousand acres of land in Ponil Canyon. He and his wife, Teresa, built a home there in 1872 that remains standing today. Chase used the Ponil ranch as headquarters for his far flung stock raising activities. The operation was passed to his sons and continues under the management of one of his descendants.

C.M. Chase was an editor of a Vermont newspaper and Manly Chase's cousin. He visited his relative in the Ponil Canyon in 1881. During his travels in New Mexico Chase sent periodic reports that were published for readers back in Vermont. The reports covered a variety of topics concerning New Mexico Territory including observations about its people, economic activity, architecture and social customs. Most of the dispatches were composed in Cimarron and pertain to life in the town at the time.

Readers are directed to Ruth Armstrong's *The Chases of Cimarron* (1981) for a comprehensive treatment of the family and its activities.

Manly M. Chase. Photograph courtesy of New Mexico Farm & Ranch Heritage Museum.

In Cimarron, New Mexico

by C.M. Chase, from *The Editor's Run in New Mexico and Colorado*
Montpelier, Vermont: Argus and Patriot Book and Job Printing
House, 1882, pp. 47–56

Cimarron, N.M., October 18, 1881.

On arriving here last Saturday evening we found S.M.
Folsom, who left Lyndonville three weeks ago, stopping at the
residence of M.M. Chase, taking his first lesson in cattle raising.
Before embarking extensively in the cattle business, Folsom
concluded to devote a season to learning the business, and has
shown discretion in securing one of the most successful stock men
in the country for an instructor.

Mr. Chase is a man 45 years old, and a border life experience
of 30 years has given him the best qualifications for stock raising in
a new country. Mr. Chase was born in Wisconsin, and his father,
W.C. Chase, a native of Bradford, Vt., being an extensive stock
broker, put him into the business of handling stock early in life.
Before Colorado had made much pretension as a territory even,
M.M. emigrated to the far West, and took a hand in corraling
Indians, hunting game, mining, etc. His business took him over a
large part of the country from the Black Hills to Santa Fe, New
Mexico. For a number of years he was engaged in the freighting
business across the Plains, from the Missouri River to Denver.
Some 15 years ago, being well acquainted with the greater portion
of the range along the foot hills of the Rocky Mountains, he
selected Cimarron, N.M., as the finest climate he knew, and as a
locality affording the richest range and the best shelter for cattle.
He moved here, commenced to farm and start his herd. From a
small beginning he has worked his way up to be the leading stock
man in these parts. He has a residence three miles from Cimarron
village, in a rich canon, from a half mile to a mile wide. His home
place contains 1,000 acres of land. Here he keeps some 40 horses,
and about 300 head of cattle. The horses are designed mainly for

his individual and family driving, and the cattle are the property of his children, who have them branded with their own marks. Fifteen miles to the north he and two partners, named Dawson and Maulding, have a ranch of 50,000 acres, all inclosed, about 20 miles of it having the wire fence and 15 miles the walls of mountains. This range takes the natural drainage of the Vermijo river, is sufficient for 3,000 cattle, and is already stocked with a herd of 2,500. This range is about half open prairie, the other half extending back into the foot hills which contain numerous canons and mesas, largely covered with pinon trees, forming the finest imaginable shelter for cattle. The ranch is considered a sort of "home pasture," and is about eight by ten miles in extent. The canons extend way back into the foot hills, forming beautiful parks, little and big, from 100 to 2,000 acres in extent, dotted here and there with the pinons, and are as beautiful and romantic as it is possible to form on the bosom of Mother Earth. They are simply charming, and one almost envies the life of an animal in the possession of such homes. The hills rise up suddenly out of the flat land and terminate in flat tops, miles in extent and rich in grazing capacity. Though very steep and covered with pinons, most of their sides also form good grazing.

Mr. Chase and his partner Dawson own a sheep ranch 180 miles south-east of Cimarron, some 12x15 miles in extent, which contains a greater number of acres than the "home pasture." This ranch is now stocked with 15,000 sheep of improved breed.

With the two partners above mentioned, and three others, Mr. Chase purchased last year a tract of country 150 miles south-east of Cimarron, and just north of the sheep ranch, embracing about 60x13 miles in extent, containing in round numbers 500,000 acres. This ranch is now stocked with 12,000 cattle, and will range 50,000, allowing 10 acres to each animal. In ordinary season this is sufficient. The company, however, intend to allow the herd to grow, by purchase and increase, to 25,000 head, and then make their calculations for the future.

In addition to the above, Mr. Chase and his partner Dawson, Mr. Folsom, and four others, have purchased a tract of about

150,000, 35 miles south-east of Cimarron, which has not been stocked as yet, but will be this winter by purchase of stock from Texas. It will range easily 10,000 to 15,000 head. Mr. Chase has the management of these different ranges; that is, he does the buying and selling, and has general supervision, with a boss on each ranch, to attend to all details, such as hiring the necessary help to "ride the fences" — go around the range daily to keep the fence in repair — to "round up" the cattle at stated seasons, to "cut out" beef to be sold, calves to be branded, etc. For his supervision he gets a salary from each company, in addition to his share in the profits.

In a former letter I spoke of the Maxwell Cattle Company, just formed for the purpose of stocking all the land in the Maxwell grant not yet disposed of, the number of acres being about 1,700,000. Mr. Sherwin, who holds 66 percent of the stock in this company, and about the same of stock in the Maxwell Land Company, controls them both, and will allow no more land to be sold or leased out of the grant, and he designs to have the cattle company stock all the land now controlled by the Maxwell Land Company. This intention virtually puts an end to the increase of settlements in the grazing section of the Maxwell grant, and holds it as a cattle grazing locality purely. Any future increase must come from the developments of the gold, silver, iron, copper and coal mines, which are abundant in the hills. Mr. Chase has been engaged to manage the affairs of the Maxwell Cattle Company for five years, receiving therefore a liberal compensation annually, with a promise of a better situation at the end of that time. The salaries he receives for the management of different companies will, if he is prudent, keep his family from starvation. In a subsequent communication I will give particulars of the profits of sheep and cattle raising, from which it will appear that he is in condition to lay by something for a rainy day.

Sunday was the first day spent in Cimarron, but it was so far gone when I discovered it, that it was impossible to "observe the Sabbath" in the New England way. As a general rule, all days are alike here. There have been some attempts to support a minister in Cimarron, and a little house has been built for one to expound his opinions in. But the first minister was shot, the second one was put in jail, while the third one got frightened and ran away. No man has since ventured publicly to expound the scriptures to the Cimarron people. The church has been converted into a school house, where it is proposed to educate the children, and let them search the scriptures for themselves and parents.

This a country of magnificent distances, and I have been bewildered ever since my arrival in attempting to comprehend the circuit of the neighborhood. When M.M. invited us to ride to his pasture, I asked him where it was, and he said "over here a little piece," pointing with his finger. I rode over with him, and found it fifteen miles distant. That is what they call "a little piece." the next neighbor is usually 5 to 10 miles distant. Localities 60 and 100 miles off are spoken of with the same neighborly familiarity that a Lyndon Corner man speaks of Lyndonville. This will account for the number of horses all prominent ranch men keep. M.M. lives three and one-half miles from the post-office, and has the first establishment out of the village. Twenty of his horses are used for his own and family roadsters, a part for odd jobs of teaming, and others are grazing on the home place, and getting on age and condition for service. One span is used today, another tomorrow, and so on.

On Monday last we made our first trip out. Chase, Folsom, the Governor and myself rode over to H.M. Porter's pasture, 10 miles away, to witness a "round up." The cattle in this pasture, about 2,000 in number, are under the charge of "cow boy" George M. Chase, who lived in Lyndon some 30 years ago. Realizing the profits of stock raising in New Mexico, he came here from Kansas City a year ago, and engaged as cow boy for H.M. Porter's herd. He determined to learn the business from the bottom up. The business of the cow boy is to live on the ranch with the cattle, ride along the fence every day to repair all breaks, see that the cattle are kept within their range, etc. George's enclosure fence is 30 miles in circumference, and he rides around it on horseback every day. In addition to his salary for service, he was allowed to put in a few animals of his own. These animals he has just sold, nearly doubling his money inside of a year. On arriving at the pasture at 3 o'clock in the afternoon, we had several miles to ride before reaching the locality of the "round up." We found the "bunch," having been collected — "rounded up" — during the day, by eight men on horseback. A part of the men were riding round the herd, keeping them "bunched" up, while the others were riding in and driving out of the herd particular animals wanted, and driving them away to some place distant from the main herd, to sell, to brand, or for some other purpose. This process is called "cutting out."

On Tuesday the same quartette of individuals took another span of horses, and drove north to Chase's Vermijo pasture. On the way we called at a place in the prairie where M.M. and his partner Dawson have a "band of sheep," 2,500 in number, which had been cut out of their main flock, to send to market. It would surprise a Vermont sheep raiser to see that flock. Instead of a lot of scragly, bare bellied, coarse made sheep, we found a flock fat as butter, well bred, and wooled down nearly to the ground. Some of them were full blooded Merinos, and as fine looking sheep as can be found in the celebrated Vermont flocks. The Governor is a sheep man, with Merino proclivities, and when he said "By thunder, I'm beat!" he was evidently surprised. He has never seen 2,500 sheep together which carried so much wool and so much mutton. Persons who think sheep breeding and sheep raising in New Mexico is haphazard business, are mistaken. The wool men have taken great pains with their flocks, and have for years past brought in car load after car load of the best bucks Vermont and Ohio produce. They have paid high, even fancy, prices for bucks, and the wisdom of this course now appears in the profits of their flocks. They prefer the Merino, graded up from the native Mexican ewe, as it gives endurance and fine quality of wool. I have not seen a Cotswold or Southdown in the territory.

At the little tent on the prairie, miles from any inhabitant, we found a Mexican boy, a dozen years old, with a skillet over the fire, frying his dinner. Chase pointed to the tent and said, "*De ca pondo la sado qua lito bon decarto,*" as near as we can recollect, and the little fellow pulled the skillet off the coals, skipped into the tent and brought out a bag, from which he pulled out a quarter of mutton, chopped off a liberal allowance, refilled the skillet, and set it on the fire. The horses were unharnessed and allowed to graze, while we sat down on the broad prairie and took our first shepherd meal of fried mutton, biscuit and coffee. But it was good. We could not speak Mexican, but we succeeded in making the boy understand that we knew how to pack fried mutton. As he saw the chops going down in the provision cavities of Folsom and the Governor, he looked alarmed, and cast his eyes towards that band of 2,500 sheep as the only security against a famine.

On leaving the sheep camp, a mile ride over the prairie brought us to the wire fence of the "home pasture" — a fence 16 miles long. An opening was made and we passed in, rode two miles, and came to the old Santa Fe station, now used as the home for Marion Littrol, the boss of the ranch. From here we passed on through the pasture, over lonely country, entered a canon and passed up two miles, to where the mountains draw together and form a canon a half mile wide. Here we found the residence of Mr. Dawson, a one story adobe house with adobe barn and adobe corral. Half of the house had been torn away and an addition was about to be built, but two or three small rooms were left. Dawson and wife, seven children, the school marm, and a visiting gentleman and lady from Trinidad, were the occupants. An addition of four full grown men to the accommodations at hand might look to the proprietor of an eastern mansion like crowding the mourners. But Dawson said he had lived in the country 14 years, and had never yet turned the first person from his doors on account of no accommodation. "You see the situation, gentleman, and such as it is you are welcome to it." After a short call we got up to go, but were prevented by Dawson, who commenced to unharness the team. It was supper time, and all except the children packed around an extension table in a low, black kitchen 10 feet square, containing a cooking range, a dish cupboard, and a variety of cooking and hunting utensils which hung on the wall and overhead. The first appearance was not inviting, but I soon learned not to rely upon appearances. No King ever sat down to better specimens of the culinary art. Steak as tender as spring chicken, biscuits as light as a feather, bread, graham and white, entitled to a first premium at the fair, sauce, preserves, pickles, etc., flavored to suit the most fastidious palate. Folsom claims to be a dyspeptic, but furnished abundant evidence on this occasion that it is all make believe. The Governor — well, he just mortified me to death. I haven't looked at him since without seeing bristles. Folsom barely had time to remark between takes, "Strikes me a man has an almighty appetite out here; owing to the altitude, I s'pose." The Governor was too full for utterance.

After supper we all packed into a room, about 12x14, with a fire place at one end, crib in one corner, bed in another, secretary in the third, while a wash stand and half a dozen chairs completed the outfit. It was soon discovered that there was music in the company, and a space was cleared away in the center of the room, a Wood's organ brought from the entry, and the school marm, the Trinidad lady and the subscriber formed a trio for the execution of gospel hymns, which drew forth rounds of applause from a "crowded house."

An experience meeting followed, in which Mr. Dawson related numerous hair breadth escapes from wild beasts during his 14 years border life in New Mexico, and prior to his coming here. Having spent the first thirty years of his life with the cattle, wild game and Indians of north-western Texas, he was well prepared for the business and sports of this territory. He is a famous hunter, and his home is never out of sight of big game. This season he has killed in this very neighborhood three cinnamon bears, two mountain lions, several deer, antelopes, etc., and had been on a hunt but twice. We intended to invite him to accompany us a day or two in the woods, but his building enterprise prevented. Moreover, after he exhibited the skin of a mountain lion, nine feet from tip to tip, with claws three inches long, I noticed the Governor's hair rising, as he remarked that it wouldn't be convenient for him to go hunting just now. He had to go back to Cimarron and write a letter. Folsom was as quiet as he could be, with a chin going through the motion of a jig saw, but he hoped the Governor would insist upon writing that letter.

Mr. Dawson's home place contains about 1,500 acres of excellent land, and, contrary to the general rule, he does a little at farming, has a variety of fruit trees, a garden, and plants some corn. Farming was common here prior to the coming of the railroad, two years ago, as every one then had either to raise his supplies or pay for hauling 700 miles from Kansas City. But it is different now. The wheat and corn fields have gone to weeds. The untold profits on stock raising, and the ease with which the work is done, make the profits of the most successful farming appear like small compensation for the labor performed. Hence large land holders prefer to buy their supplies, rather than be troubled with tilling the soil. Dairying and variety farming would pay better here than in Vermont, but they don't pay enough comparatively to attract much attention.

Mr. Dawson keeps on the home place a few hundred cattle, growing up in the name of his children, about 75 horses, a lot of poultry, and a pack of nine hounds, which guard the premises, and are always ready to pursue the bear, the mountain lion and the deer, whenever the owner inclines to indulge in a few days of sport. Dawson is an excellent specimen of the pioneer, open-hearted, cordial in his welcomes, fond of company and story telling. He has roughed it, pinched his way along up to the present time, but now counts his land by the townships and his cattle and sheep by the thousand.

Notwithstanding our "packed" accommodations, I awoke up Wednesday morning refreshed by a good sleep. On our return we took a northern route and rode 15 miles extra, through the parks and canons of the pasture, following an ad libitum route over the plains, through the pinons, etc. It was a most charming ride, and passed scenery which I never saw surpassed away from the Rocky mountain range. We passed bunch after bunch of the cattle grazing in the pasture. They were not scrubs, by any means, but well graded up with the best Durham bulls. In this herd of 2,500 cattle, the three years old steers will average to dress 700 pounds, and the twos 575. Our Vermont stock men from these figures can form their own estimate of the quality of the herd. They have our word for it that the average Vermont stock stall fed, will not surpass the immense New Mexican herds. It costs money to raise an ox in Vermont, but here he will grow up into fatness and money value in spite of the owner's neglect. He will take care of himself, and all the owner has to do is to keep his private mark on him and keep track of his whereabouts.

THOMAS E. "BLACK JACK" KETCHUM (1863–1901)

Like many western outlaws, Tom Ketchum became better known after his capture than during his active career. Contemporary 1890s newspaper accounts of the train holdups and murders in which Ketchum and his brother, Sam, were reputedly involved did not identify them by name. It was only after they were apprehended that their exploits came to light.

Ketchum carried out his criminal activities over a wide stretch of West Texas, New Mexico and Arizona. He and his gang were periodically seen gambling and drinking at Lambert's St. James Hotel in Cimarron. In July of 1899 three members of Black Jack's gang participated in a shoot out with a posse at their hideout west of Cimarron after robbing a Colorado & Southern passenger train near Folsom, New Mexico. The desperados had established the hideout in Turkey Canyon two years earlier by outfitting a cave with log barricades and a corral near where a clear pool of water was fed by a small stream.

The posse was led by two deputy U.S. marshals and a sheriff from Colorado. Having trailed the train robbers into the upper reaches of Turkey Canyon, the lawmen noticed campfire smoke in the late afternoon of July 16, 1899. On reaching the camp they spotted three men, later identified as Sam Ketchum, William McGinnis and G.W. Franks.

After taking defensive positions, the lawmen opened fire on the outlaws. In the ensuing gun battle the sheriff was killed and several posse members were wounded. Hostilities ceased when it began to rain. During the night the desperados made their escape, two suffering from bullet wounds.

Sam Ketchum, the most severely wounded, was apprehended at Henry Lambert's ranch on Ute Creek a few days later and was sent to the New Mexico Penitentiary in Santa Fe. He died there on July 24th.

McGinnis was later captured and tried for the murder of the sheriff in the Turkey Canyon shoot out. He was convicted and sentenced to serve time in prison. After six years, his sentence was commuted by the governor of New Mexico. Franks was never captured.

For a fuller treatment of Tom Ketchum's life, see Ed Bartholomew's, *Black Jack Ketchum: Last of the Hold-up Kings* (1955).

Black Jack Ketchem.

Black Jack Ketchum in Life and Legend

by Larry D. Ball, *Panhandle-Plains Historical Review*,
Vol. LXIV, 1991, pp. 66–85

Thomas Edward Ketchum, better known as Black Jack, won a dubious place as an all-around desperado in the Southwest in the 1890s. In a lawless spree of some five years, he and his followers robbed stores, post offices, and trains and sometimes included gratuitous murders in western Texas, New Mexico, and Arizona. Not since the criminal exploits of Billy the Kid and his kindred spirits some years earlier had this frontier region experienced such disorder.

While facts about the identity of the mysterious Black Jack — there were others before Thomas Ketchum — were in short supply, an abundance of imaginary stories soon filled this void. Black Jack Ketchum also contributed personally to the misinformation about his outlaw career after his arrest in Union County, New Mexico, in August 1899. During eighteen months of confinement before his hanging, Ketchum fed gullible newspapermen with many tall tales. The existence of sharp political divisions between farmers and other small income persons on one side and large property owners on the other created an atmosphere favorable to such bandits.

Common folk expressed much hostility towards railroads and other large economic enterprises, and they elevated Black Jack Ketchum — the train robber — to the status of a folk hero. Black Jack secured his place in legend with his defiant attitude toward death while he awaited the hangman in Clayton, New Mexico. As Ketchum's body plunged through the trapdoor of the gallows that April day in 1901, the outlaw presented onlookers with an even more memorable spectacle, one that merely enlarged the growing body of lore about Black Jack Ketchum.

Thomas Edward Ketchum was born on Richland Creek, in San Saba County, Texas, on October 31, 1863. His father, Green

Berry Ketchum, Sr., was a native of Alabama but was reared in Illinois. In 1847, he married Temperance Wydick in Christian County, Illinois, and the couple soon set off for Texas with their new baby girl, Elizabeth. Four additional children were born to them. Green Berry, Jr., Samuel W., Nancy B., and Thomas Edward. Two brothers of Green Berry Ketchum, Sr., James and John, also located on Richland Creek. The Ketchums differed little from other pioneers in western Texas during the Civil War Era. They were God fearing Baptists in their fashion and hard working small farmers and ranchers. "As youths the Ketchum boys learned the back breaking work on the farm," writes one biographer of Thomas Ketchum, and "the never ending fight against the rocks and stones that seemed to continually grow themselves out of the soil." Education for Tom, if at all, consisted of the standard three R's. Tragedy was always near in this insecure land. Green Berry Ketchum, Sr., died when Thomas Edward was only a toddler, and mother Temperance followed when the boy was nine. Indians killed uncles James and John Ketchum in December, 1867. The untimely departures of the four senior Ketchums in such a short space of time left Green Berry, Jr., only about twenty years old, to rear the family. In the 1880s, he took up ranch land farther west, in Knickerbocker, Tom Green county. Tom and Sam became cowhands and sometimes trailed cattle into New Mexico. At some point, Sam married Louisa Greenlee although the two could not have had much of a family life. Tom remained unmarried.

The two brothers soon acquired a reputation for deviltry and recklessness which led Tom Ketchum to his first brush with the law in 1880, when he was only seventeen. He neglected to answer a summons to testify in the San Saba County Court. The precise nature of this case is unknown. Other offenses followed in ascending degrees of seriousness, including petty theft, horse stealing, the robbery of a store, and possibly of a stagecoach. In December 1895, Tom Ketchum passed the point of no return in his criminal career. He participated in the assassination of John N. Powers, a Tom Green County rancher, and fled to New Mexico. Sheriff Gerome Shield, a boyhood friend of Ketchum, issued a fifty dollar reward for this budding outlaw. In a letter to John Walker, sheriff of Eddy County, New Mexico, Shield characterized Tom Ketchum, alias Henry Davis, as a "desperate man" and described him as:

about 30 years old, 6 ft hight (sic), Black eyes and had full beard about 2 inches long when he left here, both beard and hair dark or black, walks very straight and stammers a little when he talks, always rides good horses and carries Winchester (rifle) and sixshooter, won't work very much but lounges around ranches, trades and gambles and robs stores or would kill a man for money. . . ."

Within two years, the exploits of Tom Ketchum began to bestow the sobriquet of Black Jack upon him and to inspire stories about him. On November 8, 1897, the Denver *Rocky Mountain News* helped set Black Jack Ketchum on this fanciful road in an article entitled, "College Man as an Outlaw Chief." An unknown writer characterized him as "One of the most interesting of the modern Western desperadoes" and surmised that "he is a college graduate of handsome and engaging appearance. . . ." With no evidence to go on, this journalist believed that the outlaw had "great respect . . . for poor persons and women, the latter receiving the most chivalrous treatment at his hands." This outlaw's "nerve and audacity are proverbial." he continued. Black Jack allegedly admitted that his death could not be far off, "but while he was on earth he intended to have his own way." Although his origins were still unknown, said the *News*, Black Jack reportedly hailed from San Xavier, in the Texas Panhandle. Other sources that contributed to this nascent legend erroneously held that Black Jack Ketchum's father was a minister or medical doctor, although there is no evidence for such statements.

This growing body of lore attempted to explain the sources of Tom Ketchum's wayward existence and capacity for mayhem. His boyhood love of practical—often malicious—jokes had revealed a brutal streak. Walter Musick, who knew this budding outlaw in Texas, recalled that Ketchum was "full of devilment" and enjoyed burning out Hispano sheepherders' camps. An unlikely tradition relates that this playful youth pilfered a neighbor's pecan grove, whereupon the owner gave him a thrashing and swore out a complaint. Tom returned and set off dynamite among the trees, or burned them, according to a variant! Tom Ketchum demonstrated a new capacity for deviltry at church in Tom Green County on Sunday morning, according to one story:

> He spied a mangy old dog on a porch nearby. . . . He hurled the dog down the center aisle, giving a wild Indian yell. Ladies screamed, men were affronted and he was arrested for 'disturbing the peace on the Sabbath.'

Some truth may exist in this story. Gerome Shield, the childhood playmate of Tom Ketchum, recalled that his first official act as Tom Green County sheriff, in 1892, was to arrest him for shooting a dog outside a place of worship.

This compulsion to play pranks remained with Ketchum as a young man on cattle drives. James F. Hinkle, a prominent cattleman and future governor of New Mexico, observed Tom at play in Clayton, in 1890. On the dare of drunken saloon friends, the mischievous cowboy "got behind a pile of (cross)ties near the depot with a bean shooter and took it out on an engineer who was oiling his engine." The angry trainman promptly reached for his gun, and young Ketchum retreated to the safety of his friends. Although the legend is not explicit, the implication is that the habit of malicious mischief masks the existence of criminal tendencies.

One of the most persistent traditions about Tom Ketchum concerns the squandering of his inheritance. Many persons regarded such profligacy as a sure sign that a young man was "going bad." Ketchum reportedly received the tidy sum of fifteen hundred dollars but frittered it away on gambling and debauchery in Phoenix and Yuma, Arizona. The young man did receive a legacy, but the amount was much more modest, only one hundred fifty dollars. Nonetheless, it was sufficient to make a start on the frontier. In September 1880, the San Saba County Probate Court had appointed Green Berry Ketchum, Jr., as "guardian of the estate of Thomas E. Ketchum," a minor. The elder brother posted a bond, with sureties, to ensure his custody of this money. Tom

Ketchum's probate file indicates that he received the final installment, seventy-four dollars, in April 1885. "Said minor has reached his majority," declared the probate judge, "and is now in a condition to receive his final estate." An inability to manage money became common with Tom and his older brother, Samuel. When Tom and Sam were captured in 1899, one newspaper reported that Berry had recently given them money with which to start a ranch in Idaho. If so, they obviously used these funds for less constructive purposes. They presumably squandered this stake at the gambling tables.

As Tom Ketchum approached the day of execution in April 1901, he reflected upon the many happy hours he spent gaming in Charlie Meredith's saloon in Clayton, New Mexico. "'We sure had good times in this burg durin' trail (driving) days,'" he said longingly. Gambling played an important part in the lives of persons on the frontier, especially among men who lived a chancy existence. The Black Jack legend places Tom and Sam in gambling halls just prior to important robberies. The roll of the dice may have served as a metaphor for the more reckless act of stopping a stagecoach or railway train. Just prior to the holdup of a Colorado & Southern train in 1897, Tom Ketchum and his followers frequented a Cimarron gambling hall. On the night before their departure, Black Jack played for the highest stakes. He lost. A similar incident is attributed to this bandit leader on the night before his singlehanded attempt upon the Colorado & Southern Railway train, in August 1899. He reportedly entered Kent's Saloon in Folsom with one thousand dollars. According to this apocryphal story, he desired to make a big stake with which to go to South America. When the dice fell against him and he lost the entire amount, Black Jack vowed to rob a train or die in the attempt. This belief that life was a gamble and that labor should be shunned recalls Sheriff Gerome Shield's observations that Tom Ketchum detested work and preferred loafing.

Berry Ketchum, the elder brother of Tom and Sam, occupied an important place in the Black Jack legend, which makes Berry Ketchum a stern disciplinarian and a devout Baptist who attempted to impose his stern biblical code upon his younger brothers. But they rebelled against such rigor. One story relates how the three brothers began ranching together, but Tom and Sam, lacking the capacity for hard work, drifted into lawlessness. Berry remained on the ranch and became a solid citizen. When New Mexico lawmen captured Sam Ketchum, in July 1899, newspapers delighted in pointing out the gulf between the respectable Berry and his wayward brothers. "As a result of his frugality," said a Forth Worth dispatch, Berry "is today one of the wealthiest men in the (western) portion of Texas." The senior Ketchum owned four thousand head of cattle, plus flocks of sheep, which aggregated an estate worth $100,000. When Berry asked to visit Tom after the latter's arrest in 1899, the wayward brother stubbornly refused. When Berry provided $150 for Tom to employ a lawyer, the prisoner scoffed and said, "I don't call that much." As the day of the hanging approached, Tom accused the older brother of teaching him and Sam the arts of train robbery and of keeping the proceeds.

The opposite sex played a prominent part in the life — and legend — of Black Jack Ketchum. An unhappy experience with a young girl named Cora, whom he planned to wed, allegedly drove him into outlawry. Cattleman Jack Potter, who was acquainted with Ketchum, recalled seeing Ketchum's reaction as he read Cora's "Dear John" letter. The couple maintained a common law household near present-day Tinnie, New Mexico, but cattle drives took Tom away for long periods. Although he promised to save his earnings for their future, Tom spent the money on horses, saddles, and other accoutrements. Cora soon tired of her lover's lame explanations and married C.G. Slim at Fort Stanton. According to Potter, the jilted cowhand immediately drew his wages and shouted to Potter and other onlookers as he rode away, "Adios boys, I'm heading for the Hole-in-the-Wall in Wyoming." This remote spot was a noted hideaway and a headquarters for the most notorious western outlaw band, Butch Cassidy's Wild Bunch.

Strangely, this unhappy experience did not prevent Tom

Ketchum from exalting womanhood. One account has this young Texas cowboy shooting and killing the proprietor of a restaurant in Kansas when the owner abused a waitress for tarrying too long with a customer. For this effort to defend the girl's honor, the governor placed a price on Ketchum's head and he fled the state. This elevation of the distaff side recurs in a story related to Black Jack's later days. Mary Hudson, who resided on a sheep ranch near Frisco (present day Reserve), New Mexico, recalled a chance encounter with this widely traveled outlaw. While Hudson struggled to mend a broken fence, a "Well dressed, well mounted" man rode up. While he had "a smiling devil-may-care look" about him, she remembered that he was "as handsome a man as I ever met." After helping Hudson repair the gap, he rode away saying, "Here's hoping we meet again." This "Prince Charming," as her father described the unknown gentleman, spent some days at the gambling tables in Frisco, then robbed the post office and disappeared. Only then did Mary Hudson learn that her heartthrob was Black Jack Ketchum.

Had the young shepherdess known more about this infamous desperado, she would have seen another side to him. While in the process of robbing a train at Lozier Canyon east of Dryden, Texas, Ketchum revealed a hard side toward females. When an elderly lady raised a car window to determine the cause of the delay, Black Jack looked up menacingly, gun in had, and shouted, "Get your head back in there, grandma." Stunned at such ungentlemanly conduct, she replied vigorously, "Don't you talk to me that way, young man." At this point, the highwayman broke off the conversation and went about his unlawful trade.

Women continued to appear in the growing Black Jack legend. As Ketchum faced the hangman's rope in April 1901, he asked the sheriff to send a photograph to Eva Prodman of Lodi, California. Ketchum refused to divulge anything about her. When Salome Garcia, Union County Sheriff, asked the doomed man for his last request, Black Jack asked for female companionship.

According to William French, who ranched in northeastern New Mexico,

> After hours of futile debate, (said French) strictly *in camera*, they (the board of county commissioners) sent word to the prisoner that there were no public funds available for the purpose (of hiring a prostitute). The treasury was low and after they paid the executioner, there would be nothing left.

The doomed man "did not take the refusal kindly, nor politely," added French, and "He sent them back word that they might kiss . . ." in order to facilitate this latter suggestion, Black Jack reportedly asked the sheriff to "bury him with his face downwards, thus avoiding the necessity of turning him over . . ." To add further mystery, an unidentified female—a woman of "the lower stratum," said one newspaper—attended Black Jack's burial. This unnamed woman "shed no tears of sympathy, (and) wasted no words of womanly (sic)," said one writer. He speculated that "Curiosity drew her there" to the graveside.

In addition to fondness for gambling and girls, Ketchum possessed other noticeable traits, some of which left telltale clues for lawmen. He developed a taste for sweets at an early age. This sweet tooth may have resulted from the excessive pampering that doting brothers and sisters bestowed upon the baby brother, according to one tale. During the robbery of a store in Valentine, Texas, in the 1890s, Black Jack inadvertently left "the surest proof" of his identity, according to local traction. "Before he left the store he took most of the stock of candy. . . ," this story goes, "because his love of candy was known to all who knew him well." While confined in New Mexico Prison after his capture in August 1899, Black Jack's desire for such delicacies soon became well known. Even though Tom Ketchum refused to see his brother, Berry left money with Governor Miguel A. Otero for the purpose of buying the outlaw some candy and other condiments. When the Otero's seven-year-old son, Miguel, Jr., visited the bandit, the boy always brought such items for Ketchum's pleasure. In a tale connected with Black Jack's days in southern Arizona, he is described in fanciful terms as "a Falstaffian robber much given in prosperous days to fat capon and flagons of sack. . . ."

The refusal of Black Jack Ketchum to accept religious ministrations provoked much dismay. This alienation from the family's Baptist faith may have been the result of the effort of guardian Berry to instill the Old Testament code in the boy. Such discipline provoked rebelliousness in Tom and Sam, and "conflict, confrontation, followed by punishment became the pattern" of relations, according to one tradition. From Tom's irreverent behavior at church in his youth to the calloused way he took human lives in manhood, he demonstrated a consistent estrangement from religion. When a Catholic priest offered him consolation in prison, this veteran train robber replied contemptuously, "I'll confess to you if you will confess to me. . . ." Instead, Ketchum told the man of the cloth, "Get a fiddle, let's dance." A love of music was another of his lifelong habits. In a moment of weakness, he did concede that he believed "in treating all religious people right . . ." and admitted that—if forced to choose—he preferred the Holiness faith. On execution day, Black Jack again refused a minister. "They are of no use," he grumbled. As he awaited the fall of the trapdoor from under his feet, he allegedly urged the sheriff to hurry the process. Otherwise, Black Jack would be late for dinner with the devil. After the hanging, one headline read in bold print, "'Black Jack' Dies Profane." The consciences of officials, as well as spectators, would have rested easier had the doomed man accepted religious consolation.

The preoccupation with perdition emerged in another story about Black Jack Ketchum and his band. While awaiting the best time for a robbery of a Colorado & Southern train, the outlaws took rooms in Lambert's Hotel in Cimarron. Fred Lambert, fifteen-year-old son of the owner, often talked with Tom Ketchum during target shooting sessions when the bandits placed targets against the walls of the local jail. Lambert was amazed at the ability of outlaw Elza Lay (William McGinnis) to drive nails with pistol shots. The curious youngster asked Tom Ketchum about McGinnis's criminal career. "If a person can do anything (marksmanship) that right," Lambert asked Black Jack, "can't he do everything right?" The bandit leader studied a moment and replied:

'It oughta be that way,' he said slowly, 'but God made the earth and He made a Heaven and a hell. It would be a mistake to make one of 'em without the other, I reckon. He knows His business. Some folks just naturally belong in Heaven and some folks like McGinnis' — his voice changed slightly — 'and me, belong in hell. . . .'

Ketchum urged Fred Lambert to continue target practice, "and you will be good enough for Heaven." If Ketchum denied himself the prospects of religious salvation, he still held to the Christian notion of dual worlds of good and bad men.

The fact that the bandit chieftain shunned formal religion did not preclude other forms of personal discipline. According to the Denver *Rocky Mountain News*, which reported Ketchum's last days in some detail, he "had never used tobacco and had never been drunk." "I've tasted all kinds of drinks and tried to get pleasure out of them," the outlaw confided in one newsman. When the attending physician amputated Ketchum's arm, which had been struck by a shot gun blast in the outlaw's abortive train robbery, the highwayman refused anaesthesia. Black Jack attributed his ability to withstand this shock to a lifelong abstinence from alcoholic beverages. The doctor was more surprised when Tom "even refused alcoholic stimulants after the operation." This penchant for personal discipline was most apparent in Tom Ketchum's practice of a crude form of self-flagellation. Jack Potter, who cowboyed with him on the VV Ranch in northeastern New Mexico, observed this self abuse when Ketchum had carelessly let his horse wander away one night. The young cowboy became so angry that he beat himself over the head with a pistol barrel and shouted angrily, "You will, will you?"

The origin of the alias, Black Jack, provides much food for speculation and has never been resolved. Southwesterners commonly applied this sobriquet to both good and bad citizens so that several Black Jacks were known in the Southwest in the 1880s and 1890s. William French, who became acquainted with some outlaws, observed that this nickname was "a favorite amongst border outlaws." He believed that it may have originated in a song popular among cowboys, "Black Jack Davy." Jack Thorp, another New Mexican, concluded that Tom Ketchum took his alias from a little known outlaw, Black Jack Gregg.

Others have contributed alternate explanations: Tom Ketchum's dark and swarthy complexion, his preference for black broadcloth clothing, his fondness for the game of black jack, and his deftness with an axe as he cut scrub (blackjack) oak timber on an Arizona ranch. Naturally, Ketchum's family disliked this appellation and referred to him as "Uncle Tommie."

The most plausible version is Tom Ketchum's relationship with another bandit, William "Black Jack" Christian. Christian was an Indian Territory desperado who fled to Arizona in late 1895. While employed by the Erie Cattle Company, in Cochise County, Christian used an alias, Jack Williams. To distinguish him from another Jack, fellow herders called Christian, "Black Jack" because of the swarthy complexion. Lawmen killed Black Jack Christian in Grant County, New Mexico, in April 1897, thus leaving the title up for grabs.

While Tom Ketchum later denied that he ever assumed this notorious appellation, a tradition holds that he once quarreled with Christian in an Arizona saloon and vowed to "take his name and build a far tougher reputation." As Ketchum approached the day of execution, in 1901, he continued to disavow this sobriquet, but admitted that the public erroneously associated him with the title. Ketchum then explained how this happened. He declared that James Leslie Dow, a noted Eddy County lawman who pursued the Black Jack band, informed him (Ketchum) that he possessed an uncanny resemblance to Black Jack Christian. Dow asserted that if the authorities should arrest Tom Ketchum, "I could not escape conviction for the crimes committed by Black Jack (Christian)." In such a dilemma, continued Ketchum, I might "just as well be hung for robbery committed by myself as for crimes committed by another. . . ." Ketchum continued to deny that he was "the original Black Jack" until death. However, Sam Ketchum contradicted the younger sibling by saying just before he died, "I am a brother of Tom Ketchum, the original 'Black Jack.'"

Given the sharp cleavage between Hispanic and Anglo communities in the Southwest, a racist aspect inevitably appeared in the Black Jack legend. One tradition holds that Tom Ketchum casually murdered a Mexican in San Angelo, Texas, merely to obtain his fancy sombrero. In August 1899, the *El Paso Herald* recalled a story — allegedly "well authenticated" — that as a boy one of Tom Ketchum's "chief sources of pleasure was . . . shooting at — and seldom missing — the Mexican herders on the plains. . . ." a variation of this unsubstantiated story appeared in *Man's Illustrated* and attempted to explain not only the outlaw's first murder but his love of gambling:

"Damn I'd like to try out my new rifle," Tom Ketchum said to his older brother Sam.

"Why don't you? There's plenty of targets around, rabbit, cactus, and what have you."

"The hell with that, I want something else. And there it is riding right toward us."

"That Mexican herder?"

"Yes, I'll bet you 10 dollars that he falls off the left side of his horse when I hit him," grinned Tom.

"You're on."

Wham! The new rifle roared and the Mexican fell dead from his horse — on the left side.

Tom Ketchum had committed his first murder.

While no clear evidence exists for such a wanton act, Ketchum reportedly told Jeremiah Leahy, a New Mexico attorney, that he murdered a Mexican in southwestern New Mexico on a bet of fifty dollars. When Leahy asked how could he be so calloused, the bandit replied offhandedly, "Oh, hell, I had to try the (new) gun and I thought I'd do it then. . . ." The source of these apocryphal tales might be the murder of two members of a posse that pursued Tom and Sam after a post office robbery in Liberty, New Mexico, in June 1896. One of the victims was a Hispano,

Merejildo Gallegos, whom Tom Ketchum allegedly shot several times as he lay on the ground. The murderer allegedly shouted, "You son of a bitch! You son of a bitch!" as he fired into the dying man.

Even Black Jack's comrades in crime feared his unpredictable and vicious nature and eventually shunned him. Dave Atkins and William "Bronco Bill" Walter, two of Ketchum's early associates, complained about their leader's brutality and departed. Sam Ketchum and the rest of the membership eventually walked out on their leader. While he and his former associates steadfastly refused to betray each other, Ketchum's former comrades remained distant from their leader. Whereas Samuel Ketchum could refer to his fellow outlaws as "chummies," there is no indication that he regarded Thomas in the same light. Neither he nor Sam acquired stature within the ranks of the southwestern underworld of the 1890s. According to William French, who unwittingly employed members of Butch Cassidy's Wild Bunch, the latter regarded the Ketchum brothers — somewhat inconsistently — as "dirty thieves and cowardly murderers." "The Wild Bunch would not admit them (in)to their society," added the Englishman. When they learned of Sam Ketchum's death, the Cassidy aggregation never expressed "a word of regret." French explained the cooperation of these mutually hostile parties in criminal affairs as a necessity of their profession. This outcast status apparently explained Tom Ketchum's independent, and fatal, effort to rob the Colorado & Southern passenger train in August 1899.

No sooner had the law placed Black Jack Ketchum behind bars than newspapers asked, "What became of the booty. . . ?" Estimates of the proceeds of his robberies were as much as $200,000, but lawmen could find little evidence that the highwaymen spent this money. Black Jack Ketchum allegedly stashed his ill-gotten gains in Cochise County, Arizona; Colfax County, New Mexico; and western Texas. While in prison, Tom Ketchum sent several gullible persons on futile searches. Black Jack reportedly informed Leonard Alverson, who served a term in

New Mexico Prison for a crime that Tom Ketchum later confessed to, that some loot could be found in a Cochise County cave. Ketchum called the particular place in this cavern Room Forty-four. Ketchum also sent Miles Cicero Stewart, Sheriff of Eddy County, New Mexico, to this same county. These elusive greenbacks were allegedly under a juniper tree in Texas Canyon. While neither Alverson nor Stewart were successful, a separate tale holds that William McGinnis, a veteran member of the Black Jack band, reclaimed this treasure—$58,000—from under the fabled juniper. Another story declares that McGinnis recovered a cache of stolen money in Turkey Canyon, near Cimarron, New Mexico. Agnes Morley Cleaveland, who was familiar with this area, declared that McGinnis (using the alias, Pegleg Sullivan) spent the proceeds freely in Cimarron until he fell ill and passed away in Fred Lambert's hotel.

The crafty Black Jack also dispatched other New Mexico officials on a wild goose chase for treasure in western Texas. In this version, Ketchum presented George Armijo, a New Mexico Prison guard, with a map that would lead to the proceeds of the Lozier train robbery, allegedly buried near San Angelo, Texas. This map eventually came into the possession of two physicians, Sloan and Desmarias, who traveled to the spot marked on the Ketchum map. When Wells, Fargo & Company detectives began to shadow their movement, these treasure seekers called off the search. They concluded that this great express empire would repossess any money found. One student of the Black Jack Ketchum band speculates that the money stolen from the train at Lozier Canyon in 1897, may have been left in that region, perhaps with elder brother Berry.

In spite of the absence of many redeeming traits in Tom Ketchum's makeup, the public still expressed some sympathy for his plight. To hang for a train robbery seemed an excessive punishment. "I am guilty for the crime for which I have been convicted," admitted Ketchum, "but I think my punishment is too severe. . . ." "There are men in this territory who have robbed and murdered women and innocent children," he continued, but "who are serving simply a life sentence. . . ." A reporter for the Denver *Rocky Mountain News*, which accorded the execution of Black Jack much (and sometimes lurid) attention, heard such utterances on the streets of Clayton. "The expression went no farther than words. . . ." said this writer, but "Many declared that it seemed unjust to put to death a man for attempted train robbery. . . ." George Hayden, a spectator at the hanging, overheard "Lots of muttering on the streets." "Black Jack never robbed anybody but the filthy rich. . . ," said one anonymous person, and he "loaned lots of us poor fellows money; (and) never did hound us to get (it) back, either." Newspapermen expressed the feeling that such remarks would lead to hero worship.

Black Jack Ketchum plied his lawless trade in an era of strong anticorporate prejudices, and he cleverly sought the reduction of his sentence by appealing to this sentiment. Great captains of industry ruled far flung industrial empires and sought monopolies within their economic sphere. The railroads and express companies were among the most conspicuous wielders of influence in the Southwest. In the 1890s, the Populist (People's) Party briefly led the political opposition to the spread of monopoly and exercised much appeal among small ranchers, farmers, and laborers. In an attempt to win popular support for his appeal of the death sentence, Ketchum charged that "The prosecuting attorney and all (judicial officers) were bought by the (Colorado & Southern) railroad company." "It was cut and dried from start to finish to hang me. . . ," he added, and "I have been told that they (the railroad officials) put money to (Chief Justice William J.) Mills and to others to prosecute me." Jack Potter, an acquaintance of Ketchum, recalled years later that some New Mexicans still believed "that Tom Ketchum was railroaded to the gallows by corporations."

That the authorities were deeply concerned about the prevalence of crime in the 1890s went without saying. Such adverse publicity retarded the flow of immigrants and capital and delayed statehood. In spite of Black Jack's allegations, there is no evidence to indicate a behind-the-scenes conspiracy against him. Furthermore, neither his family, comrades in crime, nor the public, came to his defense with any sense of urgency.

Perhaps, Black Jack's vindictive nature accounted for the isolation of his last days when his desire for retribution blossomed forth. "One of his last wishes on earth was that his spirit might come back and haunt his enemies. . . ." said one journalist. He was "Vicious, bold, and unforgiving to the end." Black Jack heaped threats upon Frank Harrington, the railway conductor whose shotgun blast disabled the lone bandit and enabled Sheriff Saturnino Pinard to capture him.

As Ketchum inspected the scaffold that he would soon die upon, he remarked malevolently that "It look (sic) good, but I think they ought to hang Harrington on it first. . . ." On another occasion, the doomed man expressed the hope that he would get his arm back when he arrived in hell, "to use shoveling coals on Conductor Harrington when he gets down there. . . ." Ketchum assured listeners that the railway man "would be with him in hell inside of six months," a not too subtle hint that he expected friends on the outside to assassinate Harrington. The ultimate fate of this man is not clear, although the outlaws did not fulfill Black Jack's prophesy. Newspapers reported that Frank Harrington died in 1903 in a fall from a train near the Texas-New Mexico border—not far from the site of Black Jack's last holdup. The fact that the conductor boasted about his part in the capture of Black Jack and received some reward money may have accounted for the outlaw's malignant hatred.

In a rare exhibit of a charitable impulse, Black Jack attempted to exonerate serval men charged with crimes that he committed. In a lengthy confession on the day before his execution, Ketchum admitted complicity in the killing of Jap Powers, in 1895, and declared that Bud Upshaw was not guilty of the actual shooting. Ketchum also assumed responsibility for a train robbery at Stein's Pass, New Mexico, two years later. Three men, including Leonard Alverson, were serving prison sentences for this holdup. In a widely publicized message to President William McKinley on April 26, 1901, Black Jack expressed a desire to work in "the interest of these innocent men."

The public grasped every memento associated with this criminal's career. Black Jack Ketchum became the cultic figure in a dark legend. William French, who had moved his ranch to Colfax County in the late 1890s, encountered a party of Coloradans returning by train from the Ketchum hanging. The Englishman, who had refused to attend this ceremony, recalled that "One refined gentleman of the legal profession produced Black Jack's ear from his pocket. . . ." "Needless to say I congratulated him," added the astonished cattleman, "but I did not stay in his company. . . ." Spectators also removed locks of the dead outlaw's hair, and they cut off pieces of the rope used to release the trapdoor of the gallows. Sheriff Salome Garcia reportedly retained the noose as a souvenir for his daughter. The printed invitations and photographs of the hanging remain prized possessions to this day. Leonard Alverson, the one-time prison mate of Tom Ketchum, showed friends a razor with which he shaved Black Jack. The Union County jail in Clayton became a tourist attraction. A mysterious carving on a rock outcrop on the Philmont Scout Ranch near Cimarron is said to be "the most perfect likeness of Thomas E. Ketchum one could hope to find anywhere!" The cave in nearby Turkey Canyon was also named for the outlaw. One Colorado relic hunter sought the ultimate memento: the outlaw's corpse for an English museum. Sheriff Salome Garcia wisely discouraged such ghoulishness. Rumors persisted for some time that body snatchers planned to exhume the body.

Black Jack Ketchum's weapons continued to excite much curiosity. Upon his capture in August 1899, Ketchum gave one handgun—"his beautiful pearl-handled .45 Colt six-shooter, belt and scabbard"—to a crewman of the train he attempted to rob. This handgun may be the one that came into the possession of Deputy United States Marshall Frank W. Hall, who formed part of the guard that escorted Ketchum to Clayton for execution. In the early 1950s, Hall's daughter sold this weapon, with other Black Jack items, to a New York gun dealer, who placed the collection on the market for $2500.

Face on the Rock

In 1977, another of Black Jack Ketchum's six-shooters surfaced in the family of Edgar Clarence Smith, a nephew of the outlaw. Black Jack discarded this Colt .45 — serial #128145 — because it fired the outmoded black powder cartridges. This weapon, too, has brought a respectable (but unspecified) sum of money from a collector. Black Jack's arsenal also included a rifle which his captor, Saturnino Pinard, acquired. Pinard passed the gun to Governor Miguel A. Otero who, in turn, presented it to Theodore Roosevelt. Otero declared that Tom Ketchum expressed a desire that the famous Rough Rider should receive the rifle. This desire may be related to the wild speculation that Tom and Sam

Ketchum investigated the possibility of volunteering for military service in Roosevelt's regiment.

The unhappy circumstances that accompanied Black Jack Ketchum's hanging and burial supplied the final ingredient in his legend. This terminal event took place in Clayton, New Mexico, on Friday, April 26, 1901. One spectator recalled that a carnival-like atmosphere prevailed. Excursion trains delivered many curiosity seekers from neighboring states. Sheriff Salome Garcia, the official executioner, inadvertently turned this tragic event into a grislier one. Not only did he miss the rope with the first stroke of his axe — rumor held that Garcia was tipsy — but the fall of Black Jack resulted in more than a broken neck. The plunge caused decapitation. Much speculation took place in an effort to determine the reason for his macabre ending. In an incredible bit of understatement, the sheriff protested that "nothing out of the ordinary happened," but that the decapitation "was caused by him being a very heavy man."

Public curiosity followed the dead outlaw to his gravesite. While journalists noted that the graveside audience shed no tears over Black Jack, the plot became a sort of shrine. Visitors complained that they could not locate the grave, since Sheriff Garcia deliberately left it unmarked. In view of the popularity of the grave, a committee of interested persons eventually obtained permission to remove Tom Ketchum's body to a well kept cemetery in Clayton. On September 10, 1933, some 1500 spectators watched as Jack Potter and others of the committee conducted a solemn ceremony of exhumation. Black Jack's body was still in a remarkably good state of preservation, although some persons present could not resist the opportunity to obtain more relics, including locks of hair and pieces of the outlaw's clothing. One committeeman narrated the history of Black Jack to the gathering. The new gravesite was clearly marked, and it is reported that anonymous admirers still place flowers on Black Jack's grave. One writer explained this sentimentality as a continuation of the belief "that Western outlaws were somehow different from other (contemporary) outlaws. . . ." Frontier desperadoes such as Tom

Ketchum, "did not rob widows and orphans." They went bad through a bad break or bad judgement. Black Jack Ketchum was simply "a cowboy who went wrong."

The legend of Black Jack is largely one dimensional, with callousness and vindictiveness in the ascendancy and an obsession with doomsday lurking in the background. One student of frontier lawlessness has rightly observed that Ketchum "was not a man to admire and that he therefore "never quite had the stuff of which legends are made." This is true if legendary subjects are expected to exhibit only positive attributes. The appeal of the Billy the Kid legend arises from the existence of a positive, heroic aspect which counters his vicious, anti-heroic side. Ketchum's misfortune was to exemplify only the dark, anti-heroic side of human nature. Kenneth Fordyce, who collected Black Jack lore from persons who lived during the Ketchum era, noted this contrast:

"People like some outlaws (he wrote) like "Billy the Kid" and others who used their (stolen) gains to bring happiness and joy to the needy. Many doors were open (ed) to those men, but he, 'Black Jack,' could think of no reason why any household should welcome him. . . ."

Black Jack Ketchum passed from this earth but not from human memory. A body of legend began to form even before his death and this corpus continues to grow. In the half decade 1896–1901, in which he either pillaged the railroads or awaited execution, "Black Jack" became a common subject of conversation in the Southwest. The newspapers, especially Denver journals, contributed significantly to growth of the legend and, in addition, Black Jack's long period of confinement before his execution gave him an opportunity to embellish his past.

While these tales are not always the happiest, they include a wide assortment of subjects varying from the causes of his drift into outlawry; to his views about women and religion; to his personal quirks and relations with comrades; and to the macabre stories surrounding his execution. In spite of the rather black nature of his legend, curious human beings quickly set him aside from the everyday person by collecting relics associated with Black Jack. A pilgrimage to his gravesite in Clayton, New Mexico, became an equally essential gesture and indicated the growth of a "cult" around this lawless man.

Perhaps, the shade of the infamous desperado is doomed forever to roam that nether world of malignant spirits where all doors are closed to them. Whatever the case, Black Jack Ketchum was one of the last western badmen to reach legendary status before the final passing of the frontier into a new era — urban, industrial America. In the very year that Thomas E. Ketchum climbed to the gallows platform in Clayton, New Mexico, financier J. Pierpoint Morgan masterminded the formation of the mightiest of the great trusts, United States Steel. The coincidence of Black Jack Ketchum's lawless exploits against the growing railroad empires and the wrenching passage of the last pioneer generation into this new and unsettling age may offer insights into the processes by which such as the Black Jack Ketchum legends are made.

HENRIETTA CLAY CURTIS CHASE (1880–1927)

Nettie Chase, the only woman represented in this collection, was married to Manly Chase's son, Mason. Her rough and ready spirit is representative of countless women who lived on ranches in the West. Fortunately, many of their stories have come to light in books and articles published in the last ten years, although additional accounts are needed to further illuminate the frontier experience from a woman's perspective.

Nettie Chase after a hunt in the Ponil country. Photograph courtesy of New Mexico Farm & Ranch Heritage Museum.

Nettie Chase's World

by Ruth W. Armstrong, *El Palacio*
Vol. 87, No. 2, Summer, 1981, pp 33–37

Henrietta Clay Curtis Chase might well have slapped her thigh and howled if anyone told her she was a heroic or historic character. She wasn't heroic in the sense that she led or influenced multitudes, but she was extraordinary and admirable in the way she met the demands of her daily life as the daughter and wife of pioneer settlers in northeastern New Mexico. She was a woman of her time and place. She could shoot a mountain lion, ride a bronc, brand a calf, console a sick person, help start a church — in the saloon if necessary — as well as raise orphaned children.

Nettie's grandfather, Joel Curtis, saw New Mexico with John Dawson and Tom Stockton in 1866, driving a herd of cattle up the Goodnight-Loving Trail to Colorado. Both men had been on Dawson's first drive up this route in 1860 to the gold mines around Central City, but during the Civil War they made no drives. In the fall of 1866 they brought the herd up the Horsehead Route of the Goodnight-Loving as far as Fort Sumner, let them winter on the rich grass, and drove them on to Colorado in the spring of 1867. They had admired the Cimarron country when they passed through it, and in 1867 bought land on the Vermejo River from Lucien Maxwell.

That fall they drove another herd of longhorns from Texas, and brought their families and got them settled on the Vermejo River while the cattle wintered. Dawson was the acknowledged leader for a half dozen families, most of whom were related. Stockton and Curtis were his brothers-in-law.

Nettie's father, Zenas, grew up on the upper Vermejo. As a teenager he was a buffalo skinner and cook for a buffalo hunting outfit out of Dodge City; later he worked for some of the large cattle companies around Cimarron and Springer, and for the Chase-Eno Sheep Company in Texas. In 1878 Zenas married Mary

Todhunter, a motherless girl who worked for the Dawson family, and the newlyweds lived among their friends and relatives on the Vermejo. In twelve years they had five daughters and a son. Nettie was the eldest, born in 1880.

One unusual and early story about Nettie happened on August 18, 1893. Her father and R.H. Howard were working for M.M. Chase at his new sheep ranch near Hansford, Texas. The men had gone on ahead to build barns, pens, fences and homes for the employees whose families would follow later. On that afternoon Mrs. Curtis and Mrs. Howard with all their children were driving a three-seated wagon to a dance when a hard thundershower overtook them. Lightning struck nearby, killing a dog, and knocking down the mule, Nettie and her sister Rachel. Nettie fell to the ground unconscious, her clothing on fire. Her mother poured quantities of water on her while the other woman ran screaming toward some cowboys seen in the distance. They drove the wagon to the nearest house where Nettie, still unconscious, was put to bed. It was weeks before she was able to go home, and the ordeal was never forgotten. When the lightning struck she had had on a necklace of small gold beads which melted against her flesh, leaving a necklace of scars that would remain with her the rest of her life.

Several living relatives recalled that the scars looked like little beads painted on her skin. Sometimes she tried to cover the marks with makeup. She sometimes wore a string of beads of a larger size to cover the imprints.

Eighteen hundred ninety-three was the year of the "silver panic" and the bottom dropped out of the western cattle market, but M.M. Chase continued to buy sheep for the Texas ranch. The employees became part of the community; Zenas was elected the first sheriff of Hansford. Nettie grew into a robust, outdoor girl.

On March 27, 1895 she and Mason Chase were married. She was fifteen, he was twenty-five. It was said that even in New Mexico she had had a schoolgirl's crush on him, and at the sheep ranch it matured into a genuine romance. Mason had been back East to college, had been married and divorced, and had a reputation as a swashbuckling ladies' man. He seemed worldly compared to tomboy Nettie, but they were well suited and enjoyed a happy married life.

Later in 1895 the senior Chase decided to move the sheep operation back to New Mexico. One reason was that most of the Hispanic Cimarron sheepherders would not stay in the Panhandle. Land was leased from Charles Springer on the Dorsey Range, and headquarters would be set up at Veda, near Grenville. Letters through the winter in Texas told of the hard, cold job of dipping 11,000 sheep in a tobacco solution, and yet losing 820 of them to scab. Others died in heavy rains. Through it all Nettie helped like a man. Mason took charge of the drive to Veda, camping with the sheep. Men had been sent ahead to build shearing sheds and a nice little adobe house for Mason and Nettie. Life at first may have been even harder at Veda than in Texas or the Cimarron country because of the isolation and cold winter storms that swept across the plains.

Mrs. M.M. Chase died in 1900 and Nettie took her place at the Cimarron ranch, spending only part of the time at Veda. The Chase daughters were all now married and had moved away or had children; Nettie was the logical one, then, to take on this role, although she was only twenty. She was kind to her father-in-law and his opinion of her was reflected in a letter he wrote to a Kansas City employment agency seeking a cook for the ranch: "My son's wife is here most of the time, has a remarkably good disposition and is easy to get along with." He hoped the cook would have a girl child about ten years old. "If the child wants to go to school, we have one a scant two miles away, and will furnish pony and side saddle free."

In 1901 Mason drank from a sheep trough and got typhoid fever. Passing cowboys found him and carried him home. Through the summer weeks his fever burned, and he later said the only good sound he could remember from that time was the slow creaking of the wagon wheels coming from Folsom with a load of ice for him. Nettie, his family and a nurse from Denver nurtured him back to health.

It didn't take Nettie long to learn to manage ranch affairs. The ranch was a commissary and bank for most of the employees. Beef, pork, chickens, eggs, milk, vegetables and fruit were all produced in large quantities. Employees could "buy" these items and charge them against their monthly wage. They could buy clothing, furniture and all housegoods and staples at a general mercantile store in Cimarron or Springer and charge it to the ranch. The system required meticulous record-keeping—down to a five-cent plug of tobacco or a fourth of a day's work—and Nettie handled it all. Accounts were settled every three or four months, and things usually came out about even. Nettie was not responsible for any part of the cattle or sheep operations, only for the men and families who worked on the farm and orchard, and the cook, housekeepers and wash women who worked at the house. During harvest season as many as thirty names were on the books.

Nettie's world was a hospitable society; anyone passing by was invited for a meal or for the night, but, except for guests, everyone had to pay. Under ranch rules even Mr. Chase and other members of the family were charged board. If apples were taken from the ranch to a cow or sheep camp, Nettie charged them against that company. Around 1904 she began signing vouchers with a brisk H.C. Chase, a businesslike woman before her time. She sold several thousand dollars worth of produce in a single season.

The sheep ranch was later sold and Mason came back to live at the ranch, helping his father and brother in the cattle operation. Mason still had a colorful reputation, but Nettie apparently could cope with it. One time he was accidentally shot at a *chivaree* (a noisy mock serenade), but a tally book in his pocket reportedly stopped the bullet. It may have been that such events accounted for Nettie's taking up religion at about this time. She paid part of the preacher's salary and duly noted it in her records.

In 1906 Nettie hired a cook named Dora who had a child, Hazel. The mother "wasn't worth much," and when she left, Nettie kept Hazel and she and Mason raised her as their own.

They put her in a private school in Trinidad, and during some years Nettie took her to Denver to buy clothes. They also raised one of Nettie's nephews whose father had died, and several other youngsters lived with them from time to time.

By 1911 Nettie Chase's chicken farm became the Ponil Poultry Plant, selling more than a thousand chickens, ducks and turkeys a year. She usually found a way to mix business with pleasure; before Thanksgiving she and Mason sponsored a turkey shoot, selling tickets at $2.50 each. Mason shipped thousands of pounds of oats, barley and coal from the ranch, and after the railroad was laid up Chase Canyon to Ponil Park, they shipped out boxcar-loads of apples and other fruit. . . .

The following year Nettie came down with scarlet fever. Dr. Charles Kohlhausen, who was married to Mason's sister, Laura, wrote from Raton to Stan, Mason's brother:

> Your father told me today that Nettie has scarlet fever. I don't know whether the children have been exposed or not, but am sending you some pills I always use to help prevent the disease, and I think they have proven effective, anyway they can do no harm. Give each one three pills a day. It would also be well to have them gargle or wash their mouths with a solution of a teaspoon of Listerine in a tumbler full of water once a day. Scarlet fever is produced by foul air, especially air poisoned with sewer gas, so take all precautions about that. Don't allow anyone or anything from Chase Ranch to come into contact with the children. When Nettie is around again *everything* there should be washed, aired and disinfected. Look well after your plumbing and correct any defects, especially look after the traps. Fresh air and sunshine are still the best disinfectants.

Nettie and all the Chases loved to hunt. Every fall they all hunted deer; in 1915 Nettie killed her first bear. That same year M.M. Chase died and left the ranch in trust for his five surviving children, stipulating that it could not be sold by that generation. (It is presently owned by the *fourth* generation.)

A few years later Stanley and his wife came to live at the

ranch, and Mason and Nettie moved up the canyon to the Ring Place which Mason, Stanley and their brother-in-law, Charles Springer, leased from the Maxwell Company. It is a beautiful location at the foot of Costilla Peak near Ponil Park. Mason and Nettie also leased the XA Ranch on North (Upper) Ponil Creek, and stocked the places heavily with cattle. Here Nettie was in her element. Raising chickens had been a good way to make money, but it didn't match living in the mountains, riding in the roundup, helping brand, and being able to hunt deer, bear or mountain lion whenever she wanted to.

In the summer the rest of the family came up for a vacation, bringing the ranch maid and cook. They set up tents and kept house very much as they did at home. The youngest Chase daughter, Mary Springer, brought a brass bed and mattress, had breakfast served to her in bed, and after the noon meal put on an afternoon gown. The other women wore trousers under gabardine coats.

The cattle market fluctuated radically for a couple of years, and the Chases lost most of the cattle on the Ring Place. They tried to turn the property into a resort camp, and published an attractive brochure with many pictures which was mailed to prospects all over the country. They called it Kit Carson Camp and advertised that guests would be met at the train in Cimarron, taken to the home ranch where they would have chicken dinner and home-made ice cream before being taken on horseback, guided by Mason or Stanley, to the camps on the Upper Ponil where they could fish, hunt or explore mountain trails. They did attract a few guests, but the enterprise was not profitable.

The venture had a more far-reaching effect than anyone knew at the time, however. A wealthy oilman from Oklahoma, Waite Phillips, visited the area in 1925 or 1926, and liked it so much he bought part of Cimarron Canyon, Turkey Canyon, Dean Canyon and South Ponil Canyon, plus thousands of acres south of Cimarron. This is the land he later gave to the Boy Scouts of America for their international summer camp, known as Philmont.

Nettie developed heart trouble in 1926, the last year at the Ring Place, and she and Mason had to leave the high country.

Nettie Chase died in September 1927 at the age of forty-seven. She was buried in the family cemetery just south of the old ranch house on the Ponil where she had spent many busy and productive years.

Although Nettie Chase's life was far from a long one, her years were undeniably full, and in the Cimarron area today this remarkably versatile frontier ranch woman is remembered with enduring admiration and affection.

FRED LAMBERT (1887–1971)

Fred Lambert was born in his father's St. James Hotel on a blustery January night in 1887. Legend states that among those sharing drinks in the saloon that evening in anticipation of the event were Buffalo Bill Cody and Clay Allison. History, however, records that Cody was with his Wild West Show in Staten Island, New York at the time, while Allison was residing at his Texas ranch where he died on July 3, 1887.

The story goes that when Henry Lambert came downstairs to report his son's arrival, Cody raised his glass and christened the newborn "Cyclone Dick" in recognition of the wind howling outside. Mrs. Lambert demurred when informed of the showman's suggestion. However, she compromised by naming the child Charles Frederick, thus endowing the boy with Cody's middle name. Thereafter, Cody considered himself the boy's godfather and mentor, or so Lambert later stated.

Agnes Morley Cleaveland, the daughter of William Morley, the Santa Fe Railroad engineer and Land Grant Company agent, drew much from Fred Lambert's memory of Cimarron's past in her 1952 book, *Satan's Paradise*. She recounts all the usual legendary Cimarron tales but two thirds of the book deals with Lambert's exploits while he was a member of the New Mexico Mounted Police. Although Larry Murphy characterized the book as lying "somewhere between history and fiction," it is a must for anyone interested in Cimarron lore.

Lambert spent his last years in Cimarron ensconced at the Old Mill retelling his youthful adventures as a peace officer to scores of admiring tourists, Scouts, and townspeople.

Readers may also want to consult Lambert's book of sentimental western verse, *Bygone Days of the Old West* (1948). In reviewing it, David Caffey, a New Mexico writer long interested in the Cimarron country, wrote: "if the verse isn't technically perfect and the sketches are good but not great, the work of Lambert's imagination is marvelous."

Fred Lambert as a member of the New Mexico Mounted Police.

The Making of a Law Officer

by Agnes Morley Cleaveland, from *Satan's Paradise*
Boston: Houghton Mifflin Company, 1952, pp. 107–113

Chief of all Fred's informal instructors, of course, was the *cimarron* country itself. From early childhood, he had been drilled by his elders in its dangers, but there were still many of its lessons which he had to learn at first hand.

One day, when he was fourteen, he set out to trail a bunch of straying horses. Their tracks led eastward over the mountains and onto the plains and then disappeared. It was a type of country he had heretofore never known and it made him a little uneasy.

When night came, he had water in but one of his three original canteens. He gathered a hat full of grass and, moistening it from his meager reserve supply, fed it to his horse. The remaining water he sipped in teaspoon-size doses at long intervals.

Surely he would pick up the horses' trail the next day! They would have found water by now. But the next day failed to reveal the tracks of any living creature. Disappointment and doubt sapped his strength.

Then he saw it—over against the horizon—a broad crystal lake with the straying horses ankle-deep near its tree-bordered edge. He failed to note that his own horse did not share his excitement. The beast, using his nose rather than his eyes, was reluctant to respond to the spur when Fred turned him toward the water, but he had obeyed Fred from colt days, and now set off at a gallop with what strength remained in him. A moment later he stepped in a prairie-dog hole, turned a somersault, and lay groaning.

Fred was thrown clear, but he heard the leg-bone snap. He picked himself up and in the same motion drew his six-shooter, took swift aim, shut his eyes, and fired. The horse did not groan again.

"Adios, old Pancho," Fred muttered. He removed the

saddle, sat down, and leaned against it. His shot had smashed the illusion which had gripped him. He knew that the water was a mirage and that death — slow and agonizing death — almost certainly awaited him. Pancho was infinitely better off.

He looked down at his six-shooter. It would be so easy, so simple, so justifiable! But he hesitated. He had never sought the easy way. He got to his feet and turned his back on the mirage.

Of the next few hours he does not like to think. Occasionally he stumbled and all but fell over a bleaching buffalo skull, but he met no living creature until late in the day. This time he was sure that he did see cattle afar off, although he was still almost afraid to believe his eyes. Shortly he was certain that he saw a flat-roofed adobe house. He stumbled on toward it.

A man came to the door and said, "Buenas dias, senor, donde viene?"

But Fred could not speak. His lips were swollen, his tongue filled the whole cavity of his mouth, his eyes were blurred. The old Mexican grabbed him before he fell. An hour later, the old man was still feeding him teaspoonfuls of water and assuring him that he was all right.

The next morning, his good Samaritan gave him a fresh mount and accompanied him back to where he had left Pancho and his saddle. He half-dreaded what he might find, but, mercifully, coyotes had not discovered either of them. It was probably too far from water for even a coyote.

Again in his own saddle with another horse under him, he marveled that he had listened for even one fleeting moment to the voice of the tempter, "An easy way to die." Buffalo Bill's words were once more in his ears, "Your gun is your friend or your enemy." He laid a respectful hand on the six-shooter on his hip.

Late that afternoon, he found his horses. They had watered at his host's waterhole, and he had noted the direction they had taken on leaving.

At sixteen, Fred's formal schooling appeared to be over. He had two terms and had completed the eighth grade at Cimarron and Springer grade schools. He went briefly to a Trinidad business college and then to Roswell Military Institute. Work on the family cattle ranch (for everybody contrived, if possible, to have a cattle ranch within reach), tending bar in the family saloon on occasion, fraternizing with the Taos Indians, who were only a day's horseback ride away, had not fully satisfied the urge for self-expression.

His life, he felt, was settling down into drab monotony. An occasional lynching, another bullet hole in the ceiling, a raid by cattle rustlers, a few stage robberies, were almost commonplace. He had proved to his own satisfaction that few bronchos could throw him. In short, he had begun to feel that he had pretty well exhausted life's possibilities, unless he branched out into a wider field.

The opportunity came without warning over the telephone, an innovation at the St. James Hotel.

"That you, Fred?" said a voice over the wire. "Well, this is Sheriff Littrell. I'm in Las Vegas and can't get up to Cimarron in time to do any good. I find my deputy in Cimarron is sick in bed, and I've got to deputize somebody right away *pronto*. There's been a killing down here by two men and a woman, and when last heard of they were heading toward Springer. They may go on north or turn west to Cimarron. They're in a wagon. Wish you would scout around and see who's in town that I can appoint as deputy sheriff. Have him call me up as quick as ever the Lord will let him."

Fred Lambert's voice did not break. "I'll capture them, Mr. Littrell, if you give me the authority. There won't be time to rustle around town trying to find somebody else."

There was silence over the phone, then the sheriff spoke, his voice a degree less steady than Fred's had been. "I'm not saying you couldn't do it—" Another silence. Then the sheriff's voice brightened: "Tell you what, Fred, I'll commission you a deputy, but you are to get somebody to go along with you. Those people are killers and the woman is the most dangerous. It's not a one-man job for anybody."

But Fred's receiver had clicked. He wasn't too sure he had heard the sheriff's final words.

A few moments later, he was in his saddle headed for the Springer road.

A woman with them! That wasn't funny. "A gun is not a plaything." Buffalo Bill's words came home to him with a force and meaning they had never carried before. Suppose he'd have to shoot a woman!

But this was no time for sentiment. Cool judgment and steady nerves — that would be orderly. He put his mind to the task.

He could undoubtedly meet the guilty crew face to face if they had taken the Cimarron road, and be in no danger. No one would suspect a mere boy, one who looked still younger than he was, of being a threat; but arresting them was a different matter.

"A gun can be your friend or your enemy," Buffalo Bill was saying. Fred reigned his horse out of the traveled road and climbed the crest of a ridge running parallel with it. Hidden by a scrubby juniper, he dismounted and surveyed the countryside through his binoculars. They immediately picked up a dust-cloud and shook in his hand. He steadied them. A six-shooter must never do that. The binoculars did not do it again. They remained trained on the distant dust-cloud as steadily as his shadow follows a running coyote.

There was still time for him to race back to the bridge leading to Cimarron which the wagon must cross. Evidently the fugitives had not been aware of the possibility of Sheriff Littrell's telephone call, the only means by which news of their crime could have preceded them.

Keeping out of sight of the wagon road, the accidentally appointed deputy sheriff reached the bridge unseen by his quarry and found concealment in the thick growth of willows on the river's edge.

Soon he heard the clomp of horses' hooves and grind of wagon wheels on the heavy board flooring. He held his breath until the wagon was across and then rode alongside of it.

One of the men and the woman were on the front seat, the man driving, the woman with a rifle between her knees. Sitting with feet hanging over the lowered tailgate, facing backward, the second man carried a Winchester across his. Undoubtedly, it was the youthfulness of the horseman who burst from the bushes which made them react more through surprise than suspicion when a stern but very immature voice commanded, "The law wants you! Throw up your hands!"

A faintly derisive smile on the woman's face flickered and faded. She was looking squarely into the muzzle of a forty-five-caliber six-shooter; a steady muzzle it was! She threw up her hands. The driver dropped the reins and did likewise. The man in the back of the wagon turned and fired, but the muzzle of his rifle as he swung it around had caught under the rim of the rear wagon wheel and the bullet plowed into the dirt at the feet of Fred's horse. Simultaneously, the man let go his rifle butt and raised his own hands, one of them dripping blood. The young deputy had put his first important shot exactly where he had intended. The killers spent that night in jail, and the next morning Sheriff Littrell arrived. He looked at the sixteen-year-old through squinted lids.

"So," he said slowly, "you seem to have what it takes to make a good officer, but next time you had better have a badge on before you speak in the name of the law."

He reached into his vest pocket and bringing out a shiny silver badge pinned it beneath the flap of the boy's shirt pocket. A formal commission followed in due course.

Fred Lambert knew that his future had been handed to him.

That night he wrote some verses on the subject, but he was no longer a child. Manhood had laid its relentless hand on his shoulder and told him that he was in custody. He had been accepted into the brotherhood of his own father, of Kit Carson, Buffalo Bill, Uncle Dick Wootton, of all that vanished host of early Americans who did not wait for the calendar to proclaim their entrance into manhood.

He had put away childish things — all but one! He had never forgotten the last vision he had of Katie Hoover and, though almost eight years were to elapse before he saw her again, he never questioned that he would do so.

WAITE PHILLIPS (1883–1964)

In the twentieth century no one has been more instrumental in bringing the name of Cimarron to national attention than Waite Phillips. He began buying land south of town in 1922, eventually establishing what he called Philmont Ranch. Starting with the purchase of the Urraca Ranch and contiguous property, Phillips subsequently put more than three hundred thousand acres under fence. He built the ranch into one of the best developed properties along the front range of the Rockies, which was noted far and wide for its fine cattle, horses and sheep.

During summer visits to the ranch, Phillips and his wife Genevieve enjoyed entertaining friends and business associates. Most arrived in Cimarron by train and were taken by car to the Villa Philmonte. Their visits were filled with horseback riding, fishing, and hunting in the mountains, often including overnight stays at either Rayado or Cimarroncito lodges.

Phillips' recreational use of the ranch provided the inspiration for two gifts to the Boy Scouts of America. A donation of 35,857 acres in the northern part of Phillips's ranch in 1938 led to the establishment of a national Scout wilderness facility called Philturn Rockymountain Scoutcamp in 1939. The second gift, made in 1941, included the Villa Philmonte and associated headquarters facilities along with 91,538 acres of mountain country for a total of 127,395 acres. The operation was renamed Philmont Scout Ranch.

Since Philmont opened in 1942, more than 600,000 Scouts, Explorers, and leaders have hiked the trails that Phillips once rode with his guests. As a result of accounts of their western adventures, many of their parents have visited the ranch to learn something of the place that made such a great impression on their children. Each visitor comes away amazed by Phillips' generosity and Philmont's great influence on young people.

Waite Phillips.

Villa Philmonte

by Michael Wallis, from *Beyond the Hills:*
The Journey of Waite Phillips Oklahoma City:
Oklahoma Heritage Association, 1995, pp. 228–236

No place on earth was as pleasurable to Waite Phillips as his Philmont Ranch. He was intrigued by the rich heritage of the three cultures of the region — Native American, Hispanic, and Anglo. He sought out old-timers in Cimarron who regaled him with colorful stories about Kit Carson, Lucien Maxwell, Ceran St. Vrain, Jedediah Smith, and all the other lusty characters who had passed through the land that became Philmont.

Waite reveled in the rich New Mexican history and the lore of the Utes, Comanches, and Jicarillas, the stories of ironclad Spanish soldiers, trappers, miners, outlaws, and the endless caravans of merchants and traders who had made the arduous trek down the nearby Santa Fe Trail. But most of all, Waite simply liked to get out to his ranch, change into comfortable clothes, and ride Dalhart or Gus or another of his favorite mounts to one of his mountain camps or lodges.

Anxious to move out of the old ranch house of former owner George Webster into what most folks would come to call the Big House, Waite closely followed every step of the villa's construction. Finally, the Phillipses' dream home in New Mexico was completed. He and Genevieve did not host a fancy gala as they did at Philbrook. There were not many city folks or high society types hanging around Cimarron. Instead, they invited all four of Waite's brothers and their families and a few of their closest friends to enjoy the many pleasures of life on the high-country ranch in northern New Mexico.

Villa Philmonte.

June-July-Aug-Sept. on Philmont Ranch. For opening of Villa Philmonte entertained brothers Frank, L.E., Ed, and Fred. Also Pat Hurley, Bill Skelly, et al. Waite Phillips Diary, 1927

Like Waite's Tulsa mansion, Villa Philmonte had been in the making for several years. It was in late October 1925 when Ned Delk first visited Philmont Ranch to draw the initial floor plans for the residence. Landscaping sketches were prepared for the surrounding grounds. Both Delk and Hare finished the final plans and drawings early the following year. Soon, work crews under the direction of the John Long Company were hard at work beneath the gentle New Mexico sun.

Villa Philmonte was built on the site of the old Urraca Ranch's apple orchard. It was a spectacular location that gave the Phillipses and their guests a panoramic view of Philmont Ranch's mountain scenery to the west, especially the awesome ridge known as the Tooth of Time, rising 9,003 feet into the brilliant sky.

Although both of the Phillipses' villas were similar in appearance, there were big differences. Rather than use an Italian Renaissance design as he had at the larger Tulsa residence, Delk employed a Spanish Mediterranean theme in creating the house at Philmont Ranch. Roofed with red mission tiles, the twenty-two-room villa was constructed of stuccoed solid masonry. Painted a light buff, the villa was trimmed in an appropriate New Mexican color — bright turquoise blue.

Outside the villa was a fishpond encircled by willows, and there were gushing fountains, a rose arbor, and flower beds thick with colorful seasonal plantings. Just east of the courtyard, the more robust visitors plunged into a green tiled swimming pool brimming with water so icy it could have come straight from a mountain stream. An octagonal gazebo with a fireplace was added in 1929. It became a place where the family could cook hamburgers and watch the sunsets.

At the two-story guesthouse built for visiting family members and business associates, a balcony overlooked the south patio. Arched doorways led into open arcades and interior patios decorated with painted European tiles. Lilac bushes bloomed each spring just outside the villa windows. Waite took great pride in overseeing much of the landscaping.

"My father could be meticulous to a fault, even when it came to the plantings in the yard," said Elliott Phillips many years later. "I recall there was a certain tree growing near the villa that he had one of the hired men transplant. Dad told the man to dig up the tree and move it. But he didn't like that place so he had the guy move the tree again. That went on and for what seemed like a long time. The fellow ended up moving that tree four different times.

"At the last spot, my father looked at the tree and announced that finally he was satisfied. Then he noticed the hired hand was grinning, so he asked him what was so funny. The man looked up at Dad and grinned. 'Mr. Phillips,' he said, 'the tree is planted exactly where we started.' Dad broke out laughing. He loved to tell that story on himself."

In addition to taking an active role in tree planting and shrub placement, Waite was intensely concerned with every single aspect of the development and maintenance of his ranch retreat. Besides Waite's personal attention to all the details, the reliable design, landscape, and construction team of Delk, Hare, and Long put as much hard work into Villa Philmonte as they did at Philbrook.

Waite again engaged Percy French, the Madison Avenue interior designer he had engaged for Philbrook, to oversee the design and arrangement of all the furnishings at the Phillipses' New Mexico oasis. French mostly used the artworks, decorative objects, and furniture that the Phillips family had acquired in Spain and from throughout the Mediterranean during their 1926 voyage.

In the foyer, some of Waite's Indian artifacts hung on the walls above an *horno,* a small native-style fireplace shaped like a beehive. Beyond the foyer, a spacious living room dominated the residence. The main features included massive hand-painted ceiling beams and silk-screened drapes with the ranch's cattle brand, the U U Bar, in the design. Portuguese carpets covered the floor, and the Phillipses added a handsome Navajo rug to honor the villa's southwestern connection. They also laid out a mountain-lion skin, complete with head, in front of the large fireplace, a grizzly bear turned rug stretched out in an eternal nap.

Pinon-scented fires, fed from tinder and kindling kept in a sixteenth-century hand-carved wooden chest from Spain, seemed to constantly blaze, even on summer evenings when high-country temperatures dipped to cooler levels. Above the fireplace, with the familiar W P initials emblazoned in the mantle, hung some of the old armor and weaponry Waite had picked up during his travels in Europe.

For reading and relaxing, Waite preferred the big living room. He was especially fond of a comfortable green chair near a round table which held an ornate lamp. A polished Knabe piano, custom built for the room, was equipped to serve as an electric player piano. The family kept rolls and rolls of music in a nearby cabinet. When the villa was crowded with people, all sorts of songs poured from the piano: "Bye, Bye Blackbird," "My Wild Irish Rose," "The Arkansas Traveler," "Gypsy Love Song," "The Merry Widow," "Indian Love Call," "Talking to the Moon," "Shaking the Blues Away," "There's a Long, Long Trail," "Rio Rita," and many others.

In the dining room, a mantelpiece bore the initials V P, for Villa Philmonte. The fireplace screen, andirons, and all the other ironwork in the room were designed and made by Waite's own ranch blacksmith. Sixteen guests could be seated around the long dining-room table at chairs covered in hand-tooled Moroccan leather. On the walls were portraits of Don Carlos Beaubien and his wife, Maria Paulita. Waite was fascinated with the history of his ranch. He had purchased the portraits because Beaubien and Guadalupe Miranda were the recipients of an 1841 Mexican land grant which included the area which ultimately became Waite's Philmont Ranch. Beaubien's son-in-law, Lucien Maxwell, with help from his friend Kit Carson, colonized the grant at Rayado in 1848, and eventually came to own the entire tract of almost two million acres.

Double doors off the dining room opened onto a patio for

outside dining, and another door led to the kitchen, pantry, and servants' quarters. Later, the main entrance to the villa was converted to a breakfast room which eventually served as the family's private dining area when there were no guests at the ranch.

Above the landing on the stairs to the upper floors and the family's bedrooms, a leaded window in three sections depicted Santa Fe Trail traders near Tinaja Mountain, a trail landmark northeast of Philmont. At the head of the stairs, a porthole window in the library, originally a sewing room, looked out on the mountains.

In the north upstairs wing were the bedrooms of Elliott and Helen Jane. Down the hall to the south was the master bedroom suite, with separate dressing rooms for Waite and Genevieve. Their pink tile bathroom was equipped with heat lamps, a tub, and a shower with seven nozzles and a temperature gauge.

On most days, Waite withdrew to the lower level of the villa, where the main entrance opened to an auto court. Located off the downstairs hallway was the New Mexico Room, decorated with Indians artifacts and a variety of southwestern objects. Nearby was another chamber known as the Trophy Room. Animal heads were mounted on the walls of the room, which served as Waite's office and den. A door on the west wall opened into the trapper's closet, which was always kept well stocked with hunting rifles, trap guns, ammunition, fishing gear, riding clothing, and other items used by guests. As far as Waite was concerned, those rooms were perfect for entertaining.

When the Phillipses unveiled their villa for family and friends in the summer of 1927, they held frequent parties in the lower rooms. On the evening of July Fourth that year, after a particularly exciting poker game in the New Mexico Room, all the Phillips brothers carved their initials into the table, just as they had done as boys many years before on a barn door in Iowa. This time, the only brother missing was Wiate. When Tulsan Bill Skelly and a few other notable ranch visitors spied the Phillips boys' handiwork, they followed suit and left their own marks on the tabletop.

Besides his family and some Oklahoma oil-patch pals, Waite entertained another noteworthy group in that summer of 1927. The party was headed by Charles Gates Dawes, elected in 1924 as vice president under Calvin Coolidge, and one of the most colorful public figures during the years between the world wars.

Dawes, winner of the 1925 Nobel peace prize for his German reparations plan, brought several other notables to Philmont that July, including famed novelists Ben Ames Williams and Kenneth L. Roberts. Another guest was well-known *Chicago Tribune* cartoonist John T. McCutcheon who, on a subsequent visit, sketched caricatures on the walls of the Trophy Room. Roberts, later known for his novels featuring episodes in American history and the winner of a posthumous Pulitzer citation, recounted the group's high adventures at Philmont in a story entitled, "Hardships in New Mexico," published in the December 10, 1927, issue of the *Saturday Evening Post*. In fact, Dawes and the others liked their first visit to Philmont so much that they returned again in the summer of 1928 with a larger group.

The highlight of both visits of the Dawes parties was their fishing trips to Rayado Lodge, at the confluence of the Rayado and Agua Fria rivers. As always, before he and his guests departed from the villa on horseback, Waite rode to the head of the mounted procession. He also brought a cook and a helper with enough provisions for gourmet meals to supplement the trout suppers supplied from nearby streams. Known by the ranch hands as Fish Camp, this was Waite's favorite of his four backcountry retreats at Philmont.

The largest of Waite's four log cabins built in the rugged mountains west of the ranch's headquarters, Rayado Lodge was fashioned of huge timbers and had four stone fireplaces in the main cabin. Before the largest fireplace was a screen with the ironwork silhouette of Waite riding his gray horse called Gus. The smoke from the rider's pipe curled into Waite's initials—W P. Another fireplace screen depicted Waite catching a trout.

Waite Phillips and one of his favorite trail horses, Zack.

There were plenty of cabinets for liquor, guns, and china built right into the walls, one of the first battery-powered radios ever manufactured, dining-room furniture made of Douglas fir and juniper pine, and sofas covered with buffalo hide. By the early 1930s, the last grizzly bear shot in Colfax County, New Mexico, ended up as a rug on the lodge floor.

Besides the main lodge, there were guest cabins, sturdy stables with wooden shingles, and a permanent house for Bob and Gladys Peoples, the caretakers who packed in supplies on the backs of four strong mules.

Visitors to the camp at Rayado usually started up the mountain trail at Waite's Crater Lake Lodge, a dogtrot cabin that faced the Tooth of Time. Once they arrived at Fish Camp, trail riders stabled their weary mounts and took to the rocking chairs on the front porch before trying some fly-fishing. With tall drinks and fresh oatmeal cookies in hand, they listened to the rush of the river and the wind through the pines. On the shady porch, hummingbirds danced in the sunlight, and brazen chipmunks darted about searching for dropped morsels to steal.

As much as Waite loved his big New Mexican ranch with all its mountain trails, fishing streams, rustic lodges, cow camps, and high meadows where vast herds of livestock grazed, another member of the Phillips family — Waite's only son — came to cherish Philmont just as much, if not more.

Elliott Phillips was just a small boy when his father acquired Philmont. The youngster had learned to ride horseback long before, when he was only a toddler at the old Highland Ranch that the family owned in Colorado. Soon after the Phillipses started to spend significant amounts of time at their ranch near Cimarron, Elliott realized he had found the place he like best. About this time, the boy also was pegged with a nickname that would stay with him the rest of his life.

"I got my name from an old cowboy and from some of my cousins — my Uncle L.E.'s boys," recalled Elliott when he was an old man. "Dad had bought up what became the Philmont, and I was about seven or eight years old and my cousins were out for the summer, helping bring in the cherries and trying their hand at cowboying and such.

"Well, there was a cowboy on the place who was very bowlegged and had a great big black mustache. His name was Melaquias Espinosa and he was not very big. Guess he stood about five foot five inches tall at the most. He was a damn good cowboy and a real good man. The boys just loved him and they went up and stayed at the camp and Dad had them building trails. Once in a while they'd come down to headquarters and I'd be there with the folks, and I tried to get in with them. They were all pretty good to me, even though I was real small.

"Old Melaquias started referring to me as Chopo. Now in New Mexican Spanish, that means short in stature, and Lee Phillips and those cousins of mine got ahold of that and the name got changed to Chope, which really doesn't mean a thing. I never particularly liked the name Elliott anyway, so I decided Chope was as good a name as any, and I kept it."

Philmont was special for Chope Phillips. As far as the boy was concerned, his folks could give away their fancy place in Tulsa and all the other property they owned. As long as he had Philmont to go to, he knew he would be happy. It was not the big villa there that he liked as much as the land. Whenever he was away, Chope's heart and soul ached for those high pastures and dusty corrals.

He knew sure as shooting that he belonged where there were horses named Monkey or Buster or Headlight to ride, where there were plenty of calves to chase, rope, and brand, where there were game to be hunted and fish to catch, and where a boy could hunker by a campfire under the night heavens and listen to the harmless lies and outrageous yarns of bowlegged cowboys.

WILL JAMES (1892–1942)

A working cowboy in his youth, Will James turned to writing and drawing about cowboy life after a debilitating fall from a horse in 1919. The twenty-five books he eventually wrote are full of stories about authentic cowboys who knew horses and cows but who rarely carried or needed a six gun. He narrated in cowboy vernacular that is authentic to the core. *Smoky* (1926) is his best known book. It has remained continuously in print and has been filmed three times.

James illustrated each book with drawings of cows, cowboys and horses, often shown in sensational action scenes. In the estimation of cowboys who are familiar with his books, the self-taught James drew horses in all poses and actions as well as anyone. Western songwriter Ian Tyson has observed that "on every page, (his horses) come alive and jump straight out at you."

Moreover, the stories serve as virtual textbooks that describe the details of cowboy and ranch life without romanticizing it. Over the years many an aspiring cowpuncher has lingered over James' stories and pictures, and thus many have been inspired to pursue the cowboy life as an occupation.

Although Will James was only in the Cimarron country for a short time, his experience there changed his life and launched his remarkable career. Three biographies have been written about James including, *Will James: The Gilt Edged Cowboy* by Anthony Amaral (1966), *Will James: The Life and Works of a Lone Cowboy* by William Gardner Bell (1987), and *Ride For the High Points: The Real Story of Will James* by Jim Bramlett (1987).

Will James and a horse he called Big Enough. Photograph courtesy of The Denver Public Library, Western History Collection.

How Will James Got His Start

by Anthony Amaral, *Frontier Times*
Vol. 40, No. 4, June-July, 1966, pp. 38-39, 63

On the bookshelves of the late Ed Springer's ranch home in Cimarron, New Mexico, is a complete collection of first editions by the late cowboy artist and writer, Will James — reasonably enough, one can assume, since Ed was a rancher and quarter horse breeder, and many of James' works such as *Smoky, Lone Cowboy, Cowboys North and South*, are considered classics of the range country.

But there is a special aspect to Ed's collection: Will James personally presented each copy and inscribed on the flyleaf of every one a warm message of gratitude.

In the presentation copy of *Smoky*, the range raconteur wrote:

To Ed Springer — a man who backs his beliefs with a heap more than words. Will James

Behind those words of tribute is a series of events which pointed James into the direction of arts and letters. Like many success stories which begin humbly, Will James was financially broke and bronc busted from one horse too many, when he drifted to the Santa Fe art colony in the spring of 1922.

Some months before, a cantankerous horse had thrown James in Reno, Nevada. James landed atop some railroad tracks and his head struck one of the rails. It was a serious injury.

Soon after the accident, James realized that he was finished as a bronc rider, so he turned to the talent he knew next best — art. As a boy, James sketched as naturally as he breathed, and always kept a pad and pencils in his saddlebags. His themes were the cowboy, his horses, and his country.

Behind the pencil sketches and the oil brushes were the personal sympathy James knew from his own experiences as an itinerant cowboy. He had ridden the trails that meandered from the cow country of the north to the cow country of the south, herding cows, breaking horses, chasing the wild ones, and living the lore and life of the rider's calling. This personal flavor James was able to inject into his work would open for him the gates of public acclaim in less than four years.

He had come to Santa Fe to observe and learn from the colony of artists, many of whom had found their success in the environment around Santa Fe. James knew he had the innate talent to reproduce on paper or canvas what he saw in his mind, but his technique was still short of the polish required for recognition.

The Springers were pioneers in the northern New Mexico territory and the family line still persists in that area. Frank Springer, lawyer and paleontologist, was one of the principal contributors to the art museum in Santa Fe. One son, Wallace, was also an art fancier and took considerable interest in the artists at the colony.

It wasn't long after James had settled down there that his cowboy and bucking horse pictures became a natural attraction to Wallace. He visited with James often and they talked of art and the cow country, and Wallace observed how well versed James was in the language of range life.

James made a few sales — one oil and a series of bucking horses sketches — but there was not enough demand to sustain him as a full-time artist. He became discouraged, and depressed; his mind turned back to the security of being a cowboy again.

One day he commented to Wallace, "Wally, I'm busted. Any chance of signing on with your brother's outfit?"

Wallace told James to pack his gear and come to the ranch. Something would be found for him to do. When Wallace saw Ed two days later, they had a talk.

"This boy knows his riggin'," Wallace said, "but he's on his uppers and I want to help him out." Wallace explained that James had been hurt by a horse awhile back and was still recovering. "Give him something easy," Wallace suggested. His brother obliged.

Ed Springer had already sent the bulk of his riders up to the mountain camp called Canta la Gruya, 9,500 feet high in the Cimarron range. Ed decided to make James a general caretaker around the camp, with the understanding that James could still work at his art.

When Ed outlined the proposal, James' expression showed plainly that what Ed had said wasn't setting comfortably with the cowboy. Finally, after some prompting, James admitted he wanted to ride with the boys—no broncs—but to help with the cow work.

Ed acceded to James' wish, more for Wallace's sake than because of any particular faith in James' ability as a cowboy, which Ed knew nothing about.

Acting straw boss, John Brewer, cut James a gentle string of horses and together they rode to the Gruya camp. Shortly after, James proved himself a competent hand. He wasn't matching wits with broncs, but on roundup he proved his worth in branding, vaccinating, and roping.

There were six other cowboys at the camp with James, and he melted easily into the routine. James drew pictures for them— pen and ink sketches of bucking horses that soon were numerous enough to serve as sheets of wallpaper on the cabin walls. James drew his sketches without models to follow, but having the feel of a bucking horse in his backbone, "those happenings shift to my brain and fingertips," he was later to comment in the pages of *Scribner's Magazine*.

About a month after James had been hired, Ed rode into camp accompanied by two companions: Jack Narin, who had a house on the Uracca Ranch, and Burton Twichell, Dean of Students at Yale University. The trio had started out on their annual hunting trip to the mountains.

In the days that followed, James made a considerable impression on Ed and his friends. They observed the sketching, and they sat with absorbed interest as James related a passel of range country stories. These sessions would begin after the evening meal.

Seated around the campfire, drinking coffee and smoking Bull Durham, James became the center of attraction with his easy style of story telling. He talked, just as he was to write, in the cowboy jargon, interestingly and convincingly. And if a story lent itself to illustrating, James sketched the particular twisting actions of a bronc while he talked.

To Ed Springer and Jack Narin, James was an unusual cowboy; to Burt Twichell, conditioned to evaluating talents and potentialities of students at Yale, James was an artist who must be given a chance.

One evening after their meal, the trio sat in Ed's tent, commenting on James, when Twichell announced, "Ed, I have a scholarship at the university that just fits Bill. It's for artists who aren't qualified to enter by usual scholarship requirements. Do you think Bill would be interested?"

James was interested, even excited by the prospect, but he demurred. He couldn't afford to go since the scholarship covered only the university fees and he had no savings to carry him through. Later James thanked the three men for their interest in him.

After the hunters left camp and were riding to Narin's place, Ed told Burt that if the scholarship for Bill could be secured, he (Ed) and Jack would stake the cowboy while he was learning.

James came out of the hills in August on the mail run from the ranch to camp, and Ed explained the plan. "We feel that you're a good investment, and if you pan out, you can pay us back."

Came September, Will James enrolled at Yale. Probably there never has been such an anachronism in those revered halls.

James studied the basic requirements of writing in English A, and had his natural artistic talents directed. (James stayed at Yale only a short time, since there was little that the art instructors could do for him.)

During the Thanksgiving holidays, Burt Twichell took James to New York and introduced him to some publishers. He met Charles Dana Gibson, then editor of the old *Life* magazine, and later saw the editors at Charles Scribner's Sons Publishing

Company. James brought with him a portfolio of his art and both firms were sufficiently impressed to encourage submissions.

James returned to the West, a retired cowboy thrusting his talents into writing and art. He sold to *Sunset* on the Pacific Coast and *Scribner's Magazine* in the East.

In 1925, James was writing his first fiction story about a cow pony called Smoky. Just about everybody has heard of *Smoky*. The book has been a classic since its publication and has been called the *Black Beauty* of the cow country. *Smoky* won the Newberry Award in 1926 as the best contribution to children's literature, and the sympathetic story about the "one-man horse" has been filmed twice in Hollywood.

Throughout his life, James would always inscribe new copies of his books and present them to each of the three sponsors who had given him that much needed lift in those depressing days in Santa Fe.

To Burt Twichell, James wrote:

Yes sir, it all looks mighty good — and to think that if you had not made that little trip in the Cimarron country and been the kind of man you are — I might be setting traps for a living this winter or else hazing a herd on the winter range.

James' letters to Ed and Jack were similar.

After the publishing success of *Smoky*, James offered to reimburse his sponsors in New Mexico with appropriate interest. Jack and Ed talked the matter over and decided that they did not want to be repaid. James' success was enough. Three men, who backed their beliefs with a heap more than words, had opened the door for the legendary chronicler of the West.

James died in the fall of 1942, and his last book, *The American Cowboy*, was his attempt to portray three generations of cowboys in an ever-changing stretch of land that is and was the West.

SHORTY MURRAY (1897–1993)

Shorty Murray was the quintessential cowboy's cowboy and he probably knew the trails of Colfax County as intimately as anyone who ever rode its mountains, canyons and plains. Shy and unassuming, he was a favorite with everyone. Shorty's story is included as a typical example of a hard-working Cimarron cowboy of the twentieth century who used a pistol mainly to shoot rocks.

Speaking of rocks, the first notice this writer had of Shorty Murray came in 1973 when I was shown a rock in the North Ponil Canyon in which Shorty had pecked his name and the year, 1922. Shorty told me years later that when he rode for the Chase Ranch in the Ponil country during the 1920s, he left several such records as a way to occupy his time while waiting for another rider.

Jiggs Porter and Shorty Murray.

Shorty

by Stephen Zimmer, *Cowboy Magazine*
Vol. 3, No. 4, Spring, 1993, pp. 30–31

>-+→-0-←+-<

I guess about everyone who has lived in cow country has at one time or another made the acquaintance of some old timer who, by force of character, disposition, or appearance, has been especially memorable. I've known several such people myself, but probably no one more notable than Shorty Murray.

Actually, I'd heard about Shorty long before I met him. It seemed everyone around Cimarron, New Mexico had a story about Shorty or at least a description of him. Almost everyone commented about what a good hand he was, a cowboy's cowboy as it were. They all seemed amazed at the immense size of the hats and spurs that he wore in spite of his small stature. Some said he'd never married, while others claimed that he had, although no one ever remembered seeing his wife. Typical of other cowpunchers, in his youth he was known for taking advantage of his infrequent visits to town. After roundups or at Christmas he was invariably found sharing drinks with friends at the Blue Eagle Saloon or singing cowboy songs on some street corner. Sometimes he did both. Nonetheless, everyone spoke fondly of him and said that his face always carried a smile. He was described as a little man with a big heart possessed of a cowboy's affection for kids and animals of all kinds.

I didn't meet Shorty until about fifteen years ago when I saw him at a CS Ranch branding that I had been invited to. He was in his late seventies at the time and still had a riding job with the ranch. I had just finished dragging the last bunch of calves when I was introduced to him. Being that I had heard so much about him, I took a spot by him while we held herd just to see what he had to say.

We hit it off right from the start, and with only a little prompting, he began to tell me just about his whole life story. He had grown up in the Cimarron country, although he had left while still young to punch cows in Nevada. Like many before him and since, he'd left because he thought he needed to see some different country and ride some new broncs. Although he didn't quite savvy the long ropes and the "dally welta" that he saw there, he had liked the country and the people he rode with. Still, he eventually got lonesome for the mountains and canyons of his native range and decided to come home, never to leave again.

After almost everything had mothered-up that morning, and we had turned the bunch loose, we rode to the cook house at Crow Creek for dinner. We sat down to the unvarying noon menu served there: roast beef, green chile stew, red chile, fried potatoes, frijoles, and tortillas and continued our visit. I learned that Shorty, whose given name was George, had worked for most of the big outfits around Cimarron, including the Chases, Philmont, and the U U Bars. He said he'd always taken camp jobs in the mountains because he liked to work alone and frankly hated it on the flats. At the time, he was taking care of eight hundred CS cows on summer country at the Stubblefield camp located almost to the Colorado line.

That's where I went to see him in July later that year. The camp was situated in a broad valley at an elevation of about 8500 feet which was rimmed by big stands of ponderosa and Douglas fir. There was a good, clear creek running through the horse trap. The camp consisted of a couple of pens fashioned out of peeled fir poles and a solid two room V-notched log cabin made from the same timber. Inside, the cabin had two bunks, a Home Comfort stove, a table, two chairs and a piece of a broken mirror. The only attempt at decoration that I could see was a few old and outdated Frank Hoffman cowboy calendars that hung on the walls.

On one side by the door Shorty kept his saddle along with the few bridles that he used. His leggins hung behind the door. The cabin furnishings were made complete with a metal barrel filled with oats for his horses and a couple of sacks of salt that he packed to his cows.

Shorty when he punched cows for Chase Ranch.

I arrived in the late afternoon to find that Shorty had already returned from prowling his cows. He greeted me on the porch and told me to unroll my bed on the empty bunk. He then went to mixing up sourdough for biscuits. I watched as he worked and wondered why he was building such a big batch given the fact that he said he didn't expect anybody else for supper. After we ate I found out why.

His horses had come to the back door of the cabin, and Shorty stepped out and proceeded to give each one of his pets two biscuits apiece. He rubbed their foreheads awhile and then sent them on their way to poke around camp and get a drink before they went back to grazing.

After we finished eating and had washed the dishes, we sat on the front porch and thumbed through some magazines and old saddle catalogs that he had laying around. He had taken off his riding boots and slipped into his house shoes. I use the term loosely because his house shoes consisted of last year's pair of Paul Bond's with the tops and heels cut off. But, like he told me, when you've got a pair of boots that fit right, you don't throw them away just because they've got some age.

Early the next morning he called up his horses. Because he couldn't see too well, he had sheep bells strapped on a few of them so he could tell what part of the horse trap they were in. All six of them were good, gentle old campaigners who had seen their share of spring and fall works, but that were still a long way away from being pensioned out.

After we had caught what we were going to ride, I watched Shorty drag out his saddle. It was a reasonably new Hamley. When I inquired, he said he'd ridden Hamleys all of his life and still ordered them through the mail like he had fifty years ago. He was emphatic when he said he didn't think that there was a better rig made. I remembered how Jiggs Porter at the CS had told me about Shorty's devotion to the Hamley company. He said that as far as he knew everything Shorty had ever owned, including his toothpicks, had come out of the Hamley catalog. Perhaps something of an overstatement, but I had noticed that Shorty had been pictured in several of the old Hamley catalogs that I had seen the night before along with several testimonial letters he'd written stating how much he liked the company's saddles.

After a few days of riding with him, I rolled my bed and didn't see him again until the next winter when I ran into him at the laundromat in Cimarron. He was in the middle of his usual Sunday routine that called for a trip to town for a plate of enchiladas at the Idle Hour Cafe followed by a session of washing clothes. I sat and talked with him about the fall work that had just passed while his clothes were drying. When they were done, he folded them neatly, but then shoved them into a brown paper sack to take them back to the ranch. I noticed that what he washed was simply another set of what he on, being a pair of button-up Levis, long johns, a Pendleton wool shirt, a black neck rag, a white handkerchief, and a pair of socks. Typical of many bachelor cowboys, he generally wore the same clothes all week, changing into clean ones each Sunday morning.

Since those days, I dropped in on him at the ranch or visited with him in town whenever I could. Not only was it pleasant to pass a few hours with him, but it seemed that at each meeting I always picked up some piece of local cowboy history or lore that I found pertinent to the present day. I was his student, and he never even knew it.

Shorty's gone now and, although I guess he never did anything that would make him famous, to me he was one of the heroes of this country. He was just an honest cowpuncher who always took good care of his cows and horses. I'll always remember his smile and what I learned from him, and I'm better for having known him.

A CIMARRON CHRONOLOGY

1841 - Charles Beaubien and Guadalupe Miranda receive land grant

1848 - Lucien Maxwell colonizes Rayado

1857 - Maxwell moves ranch to Cimarron River

1861 - Maxwell erects grist mill on ranch

1861 - Jicarilla Apache and Ute agency established at Maxwell's Ranch

1864 - Beaubien dies, Maxwell acquires Miranda's share of grant

1866 - Gold discovered along Willow Creek in Moreno Valley

1867 - Gold discovered along Ute Creek at the foot of Baldy Mountain

1868 - Road opened from Maxwell Ranch's to Moreno Valley through Cimarron Canyon

1868 - Kit Carson dies at Ft. Lyon, Colorado

1870 - Maxwell sells land grant to foreign investors

1870 - Manly Chase buys 1000 acres from Lucien Maxwell in Ponil Canyon

1871 - Charles Kennedy hanged in Elizabethtown

1875 - Maxwell dies at Fort Sumner

1875 - Reverend F. J. Tolby assassinated in Cimarron Canyon

1887 - United States Supreme Court confirms Maxwell Land Grant at 1,714,764 acres

1899 - Shoot out at Black Jack's hideout in Turkey Canyon

1901 - Black Jack Ketchum hanged in Clayton

1906 - St. Louis, Rocky Mountain, & Pacific Railroad arrives in Cimarron

1907 - Continental Tie and Lumber Company organized in
    Cimarron
1907 - Cimarron & Northwestern Railway builds into Ponil
    Canyon for logging
1922 - Waite Phillips purchases Urraca Ranch
1927 - Phillips family moves into Villa Philmonte
1930 - Ponil logging ceases and C&NW tracks removed
1938 - Waite Phillips donates 35,857 acres to Boy Scouts of
    America
1938 - Philturn Rockymountain Scoutcamp established in Ponil
    Canyon
1941 - Waite Phillips donates 91,538 acres to Boy Scouts of
    America
1942 - SLRM&P railroad abandoned
1942 - Philmont Scout Ranch established

A CIMARRON READING LIST

Armstrong, Ruth. *The Chases of Cimarron* Albuquerque: New Mexico Stockman, 1981.

Bartholomew, Ed. *Black Jack Ketchum: Last of the Hold-up Kings* Houston: Frontier Press of Texas, 1955.

Bryan, Howard. *Robbers, Rogues and Ruffians* Santa Fe: Clear Light Publishers, 1991.

Carter, Harvey L. *'Dear Old Kit': The Historical Kit Carson* Norman: University of Oklahoma Press, 1968.

Cleaveland, Agnes Morley. *Satan's Paradise* Boston: Houghton Mifflin Company, 1952.

Cleaveland, Norman. *The Morleys: Young Upstarts on the Southwest Frontier* Albuquerque: Calvin Horn Publisher, 1971.

Fergusson, Harvey. *Grant of Kingdom* New York: William Morrow & Company, 1950.

Freiberger, Harriet. *Lucien MaxwellL: Villain or Visionary* Santa Fe: Sunstone Press, 1999.

Guild, Thelma S. & Carter, Harvey L. *Kit Carson: A Pattern for Heroes* Lincoln: University of Nebraska Press, 1984.

Gunnerson, Dolores A. *The Jicarilla Apaches: A Study in Survival* DeKalb: Northern Illinois Press, 1974.

Hilton, Tom. *Nevermore, Cimarron, Nevermore* Forth Worth: Western Heritage Press, 1970.

Keleher, William A. *Maxwell Land Grant: A New Mexico Item* Santa Fe: The Rydal Press, 1942.

Lambert, Fred. *Bygone Days of the Old West* Kansas City: Burton Publishing Company, 1948.

Murphy, Lawrence R. *Lucien Bonaparte Maxwell: Napoleon of the Southwest* Norman: University of Oklahoma Press, 1983.

____*Out in God's Country* Springer: Springer Publishing Company, 1969.

____*Philmont: A History of New Mexico's Cimarron Country* Albuquerque: University of New Mexico Press, 1972.

Parsons, Chuck. *Clay Allison: Portrait of a Shootist* Pecos, Texas: West of the Pecos Museum, 1983.

Pearson, Jim Berry. *The Maxwell Land Grant* Norman: University of Oklahoma Press, 1961.

Stanley, F. *Desperadoes of New Mexico* Denver: World Press, Inc., 1953.

____*The Grant That Maxwell Bought* Denver: World Press Publishing Company, 1952.

____*One Half Mile from Heaven or the Cimarron Story* Denver: World Press Publishing Company, 1949.

Taylor, Morris F. *O.P. McMains and the Maxwell Land Grant Conflict* Tucson : University of Arizona Press, 1979.

Tiller, Veronica E. Velarde. *The Jicarilla Apache Tribe, A History, 1846-1970* Lincoln: University of Nebraska Press, 1983.

Truett, John A. *Clay Allison: Legend of Cimarron* Santa Fe: Sunstone Press, 1998.

Wallis, Michael. *Beyond the Hills: The Journey of Waite Phillips* Oklahoma City: Oklahoma Heritage Association, 1995.

Zimmer, Stephen and Walker, Larry. *Philmont: An Illustrated History* Irving: Boy Scouts of America, 1988.

INDEX

Abreu, Jesus, 14, 25
Agua Fria river, 134
Allison, John, 55–56
Allison, R.C. "Clay," 47–48, 54–56, 59,
    60, 61–76, 119
    "The Clay Allison Extra," 71, 74
    death of, 119
Alverson, Leonard, 102–103, 105–106
American Cowboy, The (James) 144
Angel, Frank Warner, 75
anti-grant men, 51, 56
Apache Canyon, 45
Archibald, Albert W., 25–26
Armijo, George, 103
Atkins, Dave, 102
Axtell, Governor Samuel B., 52, 64, 70,
    72–73, 75

Baldy Mountain, 9, 19
Balla Salado, 42–43
Beaubien and Miranda land grant, 8, 11
Beaubien, Carlos, 8, 19–20, 132
Beaubien, Mrs. Carlos (Maria Paulita), 132
Beaubien, Luz. *See* Maxwell,
    Mrs. Lucien B.
Bell, William A., 21, 27
Benders, 45
Ben-Hur (Wallace), 75
Bent, St. Vrain, and Company, 19
Bent, William, 9
Big House, 128. *See also* Villa Philmonte
Billy the Kid, 26, 62, 90, 109
Bishop, Josephine, 63. *See also* Springer,
    Mrs. Frank W.
Bishop, Mrs. Robina Crawford, 63, 67
Black Horse Mine, 9
"Black Jack Davy," 100
Blackmore, B.M., 24
Blue Eagle Saloon, 147
Boggs, Tom, 9
Boy Scouts of America, 117, 126
Breeden, Attorney General William, 52,
    73, 75
Brevort, Elias, 41–42
Brewer, John, 142
Butch Cassidy's Wild Bunch, 95, 102

Caffey, David, 120
Calhoun, A.J., 25
Canta la Gruya, 142

Cardenas, Manuel, 54, 69–70
Carson, "Kit," 9, 19–20, 23, 35, 36, 37–
    43, 68, 125, 128, 132
    ruins of rancho, 37
Catron County, 76
Catron, U.S. Attorney Thomas B., 57–58,
    64, 67–68, 72, 75
Chaffee, Jerome B., 33
Charles Scribner's Sons Publishing
    Company, 143
Charlie Meredith's saloon, 94
Chase, C.M., 77
Chase Canyon, 116
Chase, George M., 82
Chase, Henrietta Clay Curtis "Nettie,"
    111–118, 111
    birth of, 113
    death of, 118
    marriage to Mason Chase, 113
    Dora (cook hired by), 115
    Hazel (raised by), 115–116
Chase, Manly M., 77, 78, 79–87, 111,
    113–114
    birth of, 79
    death of, 116
Chase, Mrs. Manley M. (Teresa), 77
Chase, Mason, 111, 113–115, 117
Chase Ranch, 116, 145
Chase, Stanley, 116–117
Chase, W.C., 79
Chase-Eno Sheep Company, 112
Chilcott, George M., 33
Christian, William "Black Jack," 100
Cimarron, 7, 12, 13, 14, 15, 25, 30–31, 34,
    50–52, 54–56, 59, 61–65, 67–68, 70–73,
    77, 79–82, 88, 98, 112, 114–115, 117–
    119, 123–124, 126, 128, 140, 147–148
    arrival of railroads, 13
    arrival of Sisters of Charity, 28
    becomes stock raising country, 12
    gold-seekers arrived at, 33
    Maxwell left, 33
    meaning of, 7
    post office established at, 26
    reputation of, 7, 13
    telegraph office, opening of, 26
    town started, 7
Cimarron Canyon, 12, 25, 50, 68, 117
Cimarron country, 17, 35, 44, 48, 112,
    120–121, 138, 147

Cimarron News and Press, 65–66, 68, 71, 75
  "The Clay Allison Extra," 71, 74
Cimarron Range, 7, 142
Cimarron River, 7, 20, 71
Cimarroncito Lodge, 126
Clayton, 90, 93–94, 104, 106–110
Cleaveland, Agnes Morley, 103, 119
  No Life for a Lady, 76
  Satan's Paradise, 44, 76, 119, 121
Cochise County, Arizona, 100, 102
Cody, Buffalo Bill, 119, 122, 124–125
Coe, George, 62, 65
Colbert, Chunk, 73
Colfax County, 14, 52–53, 55–57, 61, 64,
  66, 68, 70–73, 76, 102, 106, 135, 145
Colfax County War, 12, 69–71, 73–75
Colorado & Southern railroad, 104
  train robberies, 88, 98, 102
Comanche Indians, 128
Costilla Peak, 117
Cowboys North and South (James), 140
Crater Lake Lodge, 136
Crocker, George, 76
Crockett, Dave, 47
Crow Creek, 148
CS Ranch, 12, 147–150
Curtis, Zenas, 112–113
Curtis, Mrs. Zenas (Mary Todhunter),
  112–113
Cyclone Dick. *See* Lambert, Fred

Davis, Henry. *See* Ketchum, Thomas
  Edward "Black Jack"
Dawes, Charles Gates, 134
Dawson, John, 80, 83–84, 112
Dawson, Will, 65, 71
Dean Canyon, 117
Delk, Ned (architect, Villa Philmonte),
  130–131
Denver Rocky Mountain News, 92, 99, 103
Department of the Interior, 57
Dobie, J. Frank, 62
Dorsey Range, 114

El Paso Herald, 101
Elizabethtown, 24, 44–45, 47, 51, 68, 70
Elkins, Stephen B. "Smooth Steve," 57–
  58, 64, 68, 74
Espinosa, Melaquias, 136–137
Ewell, Capt. (Richard), 42

Feber, Town Marshal Chas., 56
Fernandez Canyon, 45
Fish Camp, 134, 136

Fisher (guide), 38
Fitzpatrick, George, 76
Folsom, 94
Folsom, S.M., 79–80, 82
Fordyce, Kenneth, 109
Fort Sumner Indian reservation, 34
Fort Union, 24, 29, 51, 70, 72
Franks, G.W., 88–89
Fremont, John C., 9, 19–20
French, Percy (interior designer, Villa
  Philmonte), 131
French, William, 14, 97, 99, 102, 106

Garcia, Sheriff Salome, 96, 106, 108
Gibson, Charles Dana, 143
gold mining, 9, 11, 13, 19, 33, 45, 51, 81,
  112
Goodel, Tim, 40
Goodnight-Loving Trail, 112
Grant County, 100
Grant-men, 51, 55
Gregg, Black Jack, 100
Griego, Francisco "Pancho," 54–55, 66,
  68, 70, 74
  death of, 69
Griego, Luis, 74
Grier, Major, 41

Hall, Deputy U.S. Marshall Frank W., 106
"Hardships in New Mexico," 134
Hare (landscape designer, Villa
  Philmonte), 130–131
Harrington, Frank, 105
Hart, Squire T., 27–28, 31
Harwood, Reverend Thomas, 51
Hayden, George, 104
Hayes, President (Rutherford B.), 75
Herberger's saloon, 47
Highland Ranch (Colorado), 136
Hinkle, James F., 93
Hoehne, William, 24, 31, 33
Holbrook, Sergt. Leigh, 40
Holly, Charles F., 33
Hoover, Katie, 125
Horsehead Route, 112
Howard, R.H., 113
Howbert, Irving, 22, 25, 27
Hudson, Mary, 96
Huntington, Collis P., 64, 74
Hurley, Pat, 130

Idle Hour Cafe, 150
Indian agency, 24
Indian slaves, 26

Inman, Col. Henry J., 9, 21–23, 25–27, 30
James, Will, 138, *139*, 140–144
   American Cowboy, The, 144,
   Cowboys North and South, 140
   death of, 144
   Lone Cowboy, 140
   Smoky, 138, 140, 144
Jicarilla Apache Indians, 8, *8*, 20, 33, 37,
   40, 46, 52, 68, 128
John Long Company, 130
Jones, Calvin, 25, 31–32
Judd, Captain, 40

Kennedy, Charles, 44–49
Ketchum, Elizabeth, 91
Ketchum, Green Berry, Jr., 91, 93–95,
   103
Ketchum, Green Berry, Sr., 91
Ketchum, Mrs. Green Berry, Sr.
   (Temperance Wydick), 91
Ketchum, James, 91
Ketchum, John, 91
Ketchum, Nancy B., 91
Ketchum, Samuel W., 88–89, 91, 94–95,
   101–102, 107
   death of, 102
Ketchum, Mrs. Samuel W. (Louisa
   Greenlee), 91
Ketchum, Thomas Edward "Black
   Jack," 88–110, *89, 107*
   arm amputated, 99
   birth of, 90
   body exhumed, 108
   commits first murder, 101
   Cora, involvement with, 95
   death of, 90, 94, 96, 107–108
   first brush with law, 91
   legend of, 92
   message to President McKinley, 105
   weapons of, 106–107
Keyes, A.S.B., 25
Kinney, Charles, 41
Kit Carson Camp, 117
Kit Carson Mesa, 20
Kohlhausen, Dr. Charles, 116
Kohlhausen, Laura, 116

Lambert, Fred, 69, 98–99, 119–125, *120,*
   birth of, 119
Lambert, Henry, 69, 89
Las Animas, Colorado, 56
Las Vegas Gazette, 53
Lay, Elza. *See* McGinnis, William

Leahy, Jeremiah, 101
LeDuc, Maurice, 30
Lee, John D., 24–25
Lee, Judge William D., 52
Leroux (guide), 37–38
Liberty, New Mexico, post office robbery,
   101
Lincoln County War, 62, 74
Littrell, Sheriff, 123–125
Littrol, Marion, 84
Lone Cowboy (James), 140
Long (John, contractor, Villa Philmonte),
   131
Longwill, Dr. R.H., 67, 70, 73
Low, William, 53–54
Lozier Canyon train robbery, 96, 103

Maxwell Cattle Company, *12*, 81
Maxwell Claim, 57
Maxwell, Deluvina, 26
Maxwell Land Grant, 7–9, *11*, 51–52, 55–
   57, 61, 67, 71–72, 81
Maxwell Land Grant Company, *10*, 11,
   33, 50, 61–62, 64–65, 71, 74–75, 81, 117
Maxwell, Lucien B., 7, 9, 17–34, *18*, 42,
   55, 77, 112, 128, 132
   birth of, 19
   character of, 29–32
   death of, 34
   first postmaster, Cimarron, 26
   home of, 21–23, *22*, 62
   interest in race horses, 27
   marriage of daughter, 25
   mill, 8, *8*, 24, 119
   mining, 9, 19
   mother of, 19
   ranch, 8–9, 11, 19, 21, 23, 26–27, 30, 35
   store, 8–9, 31
Maxwell, Mrs. Lucien B. (Luz Beaubien),
   19
Maxwell, Virginia, 25
McCullough, John, 67
McCutcheon, John T., 134
McGinnis, William, 88–89, 98, 103
McKinley, President William, 105
McMains, Reverend O.P., 12, 50–58, *50*
McPherson, Ada, 62. *See also* Morley,
   Mrs. William Raymond
McPherson, Thomas, 66
McPherson, Mrs. Thomas (Bright Eyes),
   66
McPherson, Mrs. Marcus (Mary Tibbles),
   66, 74

Menard, Pierre, 19
Mexican-Americans, 21, 25–26, 33–34
mill, Maxwell's, 8, *8*, 24, 119
Mills, Melvin W., 48–49, 67, 70, 73
Mills, Chief Justice William J., 104
Miranda, Guadalupe, 8, 132
Missouri Stage Company, 26
Moore, Captain Francis, 72–73
Mora, 25, 53
Mora County District Court, 52
Moreno creek, 45
Moreno Valley, 44–46, 53
Morley, Agnes, 66, 76. *See also* Cleaveland, Agnes Morley
Morley, William Raymond, 61–62, 65, 67, 70–72, 74–75, 119
    birth of, 62
    death of, 75
Morley, Mrs. William Raymond (Ada McPherson), 62, 67–68, 71, 74–76
Murphy, Larry, 17, 119
Murray, George "Shorty," 145, *146*, 147–151, *149*
Musick, Walter, 92

Narin, Jack, 142–143
Navajo Indians, 23, 26
New Mexico Mounted Police, 119, *120*
New Mexico Prison, 97
New Mexico Territory, 8, 77
New, William, 40
New York Sun, 68
No Life for a Lady (Cleaveland), 76
Noble, John W., 57

Old Mill, 119. *See also* Maxwell, Lucien B., mill
Olympic dance hall, Las Animas, Colorado, 56
Osha Pass, 45
Otero, 56
Otero, Governor Miguel A., 63, 97, 107
Otero, Miguel, Jr., 97

Palen, Judge Joseph G., 64–65, 68, 73
Palo Flechado Pass, 45, 48, 73
Parke, John G., 20
Parks, Judge Samuel, 53
Peoples, Bob, 135
Peoples, Gladys, 135
Philbrook, 128, 131
Phillips, Ed, 130
Phillips, Elliott "Chope," 131, 133, 136–137

Phillips, Frank, 130
Phillips, Fred, 130
Phillips, L.E., 130
Phillips, Lee, 137
Phillips, Waite, 117, 126–137, *127*, *135*
Phillips, Mrs. Waite (Genevieve), 126, 128
Philmont, 117, 134, 148
Philmont Ranch, 126, 128, 130, 132
Philmont Scout Ranch, 17, 106, 126
Philturn Rockymountain Scoutcamp, 126
Pinard, Sheriff Saturnino, 105, 107
pistoleros, 64, 66, 76
Ponil Canyon, 77, 117–118, 145
Ponil country, *111*
Ponil Park, 116–117
Ponil Poultry Plant, 116
Ponil River, 25, 52
Porter, H.M., 82
Porter, Jiggs, *146*, 150
Potter, Jack, 95, 99, 104, 108
Powers, Jap, 105
Powers, John N., 91

railroads, 13, 33, 61–64, 75–76, 86, 88, 90, 104, 110, 116, 119
ranching, 7–9, 11–12, 19–21, 24–28, 33–34, 43, 51, 55–57, 61–62, 64–65, 76–77, 79–86, 91–92, 94–95, 104, 111–118, 126, 128, 136, 138, 140–141, 145, 147–151
Rayado, 7, 20–21, 25, 31, 37–38, *37*, 40–43, 126, 132, 134, 136
Rayado Lodge, 126, 134–135
Rayado Ranch, 9, 35
Red River, 41, 51
Rinehart, Isaiah, 53
Ring Place, 117–118
Rio Abajo, 43
Roberts, Kenneth L., 134
Roosevelt, Theodore, 107
Roswell Military Institute, 123

San Saba County Court, 91, 93
Sangre de Cristo Mountains, 7, 9, 19, 46
Santa Fe art colony, 140–141
Santa Fe New Mexican, 24, 26, 29, 56
Santa Fe Ring, 61–62, 64–68, 70–76
Santa Fe Trail, 7–8, 63, 128, 133
Satan's Paradise (Cleaveland), 76, 119
Saturday Evening Post, 134
Schurz, Secretary of the Interior Carl, 75
Scribner's Magazine, 142, 144
Shelby, V.S., 24
Sherwin, Mr. (Frank R.), 81

Shield, Sheriff Gerome, 91, 94
Sisters of Charity, 28
Skelly, Bill, 130, 133
Smith, Edgar Clarence, 107
Smith, Jedediah, 128
Smoky (James), 138, 140, 144
Southern Pacific Railroad, 64
Spiers, Sheriff, 56
Springer, 112, 115, 122–124
Springer, Charles, 12, 14, 114, 117
Springer, Ed, 140–143
Springer, Judge Francis, 74–75
Springer, Frank W., 12, 14, 52, 62, 65, 68, 71–72, 74, 76, 141
Springer, Mrs. Frank W., 74. *See also* Bishop, Josephine
Springer, Mary, 117
Springer, Wallace, 141
St. James Hotel, 14, 48, 54–55, 59, 66, 69, *69*, 88, 98, 103, 119, 123
St. Louis, Rocky Mountain, & Pacific train, *13*
St. Vrain, Ceran, 9, 128
Stein's Pass, New Mexico, train robbery, 105
Stevens, Ben, 72
Stewart, Miles Cicero, 103
Stockton, Tom, 112
Stubblefield camp, 148
Sugarite Valley, 65
Sullivan, Pegleg. *See* McGinnis, William
Sunset, 144

Taft, US Attorney General Alphonso, 67
Taos, 19–20, 24–25, 35, 37, 39–42, 45–46, 53–54, 73
Taos County, 53, 70
Taos Indians, 123
Taos Revolt, 19
Taos Trail, 45
Taylor Crossing, 45
Taylor, Lieut., 41
Thorpe, Jack, 100
Tinaja Mountain, 133
Tinnie, 95
Tolby, Reverend F.J. (or T.J.), 12, 50–52, 56, 67, 70, 73
Tooth of Time, 130, 136
Trinchero River, 41
Truax, James, 24
Tunstall, John Henry, 74
Turkey Canyon, 88–89, 103, 106, 117
Twichell, Burton, 142–144

Tyson, Ian, 138

U U Bar Ranch, 131, 148
Union County, 90
Union County jail, 106
United States Supreme Court land grant decision, 12
Urraca (Uracca) Ranch, 126, 130, 142
Ute Creek, 89
Ute (Moache) Indians, 8, 33, 35, 52, 68, 128

Valdez (Rayado resident), 25
Vega, Cruz, 52–54, 68–70
Vermejo, 73, 112–113
Vermejo River, 52, 80, 112
Vermijo pasture, 83
Vigilantes, the, 54
Villa Philmonte, 126, 128, *129*, 130–132
Villalpando, Rosa, 45
VV Ranch, 99

Waldo, Henry L., 53, 73
Walker, John, 92
Walker, William R., 25, 28–29, 31
Wallace, General Lew, 75
Walter, William "Bronco Bill," 102
Weatherhead, Saml., 41–42
Webster, George, 128
Welborn, Adelina, 27
Wells, Fargo & Company, 103
White, Mr. and Mrs. (killed by Jicarilla Apache Indians), 37–39
Wild West Show, 119
Williams, Ben Ames, 134
Williams, Emory, 24
Williams, Jack. *See* Christian, William "Black Jack"
Williamson, Hon. J.A., 57–58
Wilson, Brownlow, 14
Wootton, Dick, 9, 125

XA Ranch, 117

Yale University, 142–143

CONTENTS

Introduction by Stephen Zimmer / **7**

Lucien Maxwell (1818–1875) / **17**
    Master of the Cimarron: Lucien B. Maxwell by Lawrence R. Murphy / **19**

Kit Carson (1809–1868) / **35**
    On the Rayado by Christopher "Kit" Carson / **37**

Charles Kennedy (?–1871) / **44**
    A Head for Decoration by Tom Hilton / **44**

O.P. McMains (1840–1899) / **50**
    Ministers of the Gospel by William A. Keleher / **51**

Clay Allison (1841–1887) / **59**
    Clay Allison's Cimarron by Norman Cleaveland / **61**

Manly M. Chase (1842–1915) / **77**
    In Cimarron, New Mexico by C.M. Chase / **79**

Thomas E. "Black Jack" Ketchum (1863–1901) / **88**
    Black Jack Ketchum in Life and Legend by Larry D. Ball / **90**

Henrietta Clay Curtis Chase (1880–1927) / **111**
    Nettie Chase's World by Ruth W. Armstrong / **112**

Fred Lambert (1887–1971) / **119**
    The Making of a Law Officer by Agnes Morley Cleaveland / **121**

Waite Phillips (1883–1964) / **126**
    Villa Philmonte by Michael Wallis / **128**

Will James (1892–1942) / **138**
    How Will James Got His Start by Anthony Amaral / **140**

Shorty Murray (1897–1993) / **145**
    Shorty by Stephen Zimmer / **147**

A Cimarron Chronology / **152**

A Cimarron Reading List / **154**

Index / **156**